Management Strategies
for
Developing Critical Thinking Skills

Instructional Strategies

Developing Critical Thinking Skills

Management Strategies
for
Developing Critical Thinking Skills

Dr. S. Srikanta Swamy
Professor of Education
IASE, R.V. Teachers College
Bangalore

ANMOL PUBLICATIONS PVT. LTD.
NEW DELHI - 110 002 (INDIA)

ANMOL PUBLICATIONS PVT. LTD.
4374/4B, Ansari Road, Daryaganj
New Delhi - 110 002
Ph.: 23261597, 23278000
Visit us at: www.anmolpublications.com

Management Strategies for Developing Critical Thinking Skills

First Published, 2005

ISBN 81-261-2439-3

PRINTED IN INDIA

Published by J.L. Kumar for Anmol Publications Pvt. Ltd., New Delhi - 110 002 and Printed at Mehra Offset Press, Delhi.

CONTENTS

FOREWORD

It is a happy augury to know that valuable empirical studies are being published now. Ever since the National Policy of Education (1986) and its subsequent revisions during the 1991/1992 there has been an all time effort and emphasis given to the capacity building of teachers at all levels. What may be the reason for this? Researches and recent surveys has revealed that Teacher is the most important factor in the system. The Teacher forms the kingpin in the process of bringing about change. Day by day the millennium in heading towards technological supports in all fields including Education. Technology is the product of mankind's effort in greater accountability in doing things and bring about quality in education. In recent years especially after the Yash Pal Committee report (1995), "Learning without tears" two things are projected very strongly. One is the need to have meaningful and quality education and second is the train the teachers and build capacity in them to act as promoters and practitioners of Quality. In this task the role of teacher educators is invaluable. It is at this appropriate juncture this researcher has endeavoured to develop a programme of Critical Thinking skills for the science teachers. Critical thinking skill being a higher cognitive ability to achieve quality. Hence this study is a very relevant and needed research for the teaching fraternity in general and science teachers in particular.

"Success comes to those who dare and act," —so goes the saying. Daring initiatives and changes are needed in the field of education the pre-service teachers should be diligent enough to follow these acts and endeavours to reach and meet the needs of the present society. The scientific studies should be read and understood and with needed modifications be practised. Only then we become professionals. Teachers are the change agents and if we desire to have Quality in Education it is necessary that we have improved techniques of thinking. Who else, can transform the individuals to thinking citizens than an enthusiastic Teacher?

Thinking is the most precious cognitive ability with which man is elevated among all animals. Thinking has several kinds and each kind has several components. This book has given a clear analysis of the different kinds of Thinking and focuses on the importance of CRITICAL THINKING. It has on focus for its empirical study, only the science teachers (Trainees). The researcher has made an indepth analysis of the factors and components that could easily be trained. Though the sample chosen for the study is physical science students and prospective teachers, the design of the program gives enough scope for generating the skill in any subject. The merit of the study is in the development and validation of a program to enrich the ability of critical thinking and a tool to measure the same. The tool could be used for any content, but components of thinking will be the same. I wish the teacher trainers catch this point and prepare many modules for training teachers in many subjects. Dr. Srikantaswamy deserves congratulations for this contribution which has lot of potential applications.

A cognitive ability is trainable is a known fact. The attempt to prepare a model and put it into use is a daring effort. It is time to popularize modules like this and after several tryouts, it is possible to standardize the tools and model with local access for flexibility. The six components selected viz. Distinguishing the relevant from irrelevant information, Determining the factual accuracy of a statement,

Determining the credibility of a source, Identifying unstated assumptions, Determining the strength of an argument and Distinguishing between verifiable facts from value claims are key to any situation of problem solving and Decision making in policy matters.

A program of Critical Thinking like this, if converted to a self learning (SLM) with alternate situations. (General), in fact, may be taken by every administrator and politician for professional growth and capacity building. I suggest the researcher Dr. Srikantaswamy could further his research to reach all concerned. It could be made useful for more teachers in the fraternity by preparing several SLMs parallel. I strongly recommend the POCTS program to be introduced under methodology of teaching sciences in the training colleges. The scoring of the tool prepared is significant and ardent researchers would surely appreciate this work which is an outcome of scientific thinking and has several positive indicators for wider applicability. I wish the readers to be observant of many conclusions and relations built in this study. May the scientific thinkers draw more and more lessons out of this and become true thinkers of this century. All the social issues would remain solved if only many of us develop the right kind of thinking and especially the art of Critical Thinking skills. This book is recommended for all the colleges of education.

May the beauty of reasoning touch and transform your hearts and hence may teaching become a pleasurable task.

Dr. Jayalakshmi T.K.
Director
R.V. Educational Consortium

ACKNOWLEDGEMENT

Research is a cooperative endeavour. In this, the researcher has to seek lot of guidance and cooperation from various persons to complete the research work.

I wish to express my sincere gratitude to Dr. Chinnappa (Dean, Faculty of Education), Dr. M. Khajapeer (Former Dean) and Dr. S. Puranik (Chairman, P.G. Department of Education) for their continuous encouragement and guidance.

I sincerely express my heartfelt thanks to my guide Dr. T.K. Jayalakshmi (Professor and Principal, R.V. Teachers College) who has been a source of inspiration in carrying out this research. Without her expertise, guidance and encouragement, it would not have been possible to complete this work. I also thank Dr. D. Shivappa, Dr. D. S. Shivananda and all the staff members of the P.G. Department of Education, Bangalore University for their encouragement.

I wish to thank Dr. C. Madhukar, Dr. S Bhaskara, Dr. H.S. Nagaraj, Sri. Ramachandra Shastry and Sri. Madhusudan for their advice and suggestions, regarding the development of the programme for the research. I also thank the Principals, Prof. T.L. Krishna, Prof. Shantha Diwakar, Prof. Puttaramaiah and Prof. Susheela Seshadri and all the staff members and trainees of various colleges of Education who have helped in completing this research.

I wish to thank sincerely all the staff members of R.V. Teachers College for their kind support and encouragement.

It is my duty to thank profoundly Dr. C.S. Nagaraj, Reader, ISEC and Sri Satishchandra for their technical guidance regarding the Analysis of Data.

I sincerely express my gratitude to Prof. A.S. Nanjundaswamy and Sri. S.V. Mohankumar for their kind suggestions and guidance regarding effective presentation of the research report.

I wish to thank and appreciate the author Barry K. Beyar, whose work has really inspired and given insight regarding the present research.

I would like to thank the technical experts who have computed my data and given out an attractive output of my research. In this direction, I sincerely express my gratitude to Sri. T.V. Anilkuma, Sri. Kailash Negharaj (JMHS), Sri Basavaraj, Rudrappa, Sri. Ananth, Sri. Raviprasad and Sri. K.S. Radha Krishna.

I express my sincere gratitude to Mr. J.L. Kumar, Managing Director, Anmol Publications Pvt. Ltd. and Sri V. Srinivasa Murthy for their encouragement and support.

Lastly, I express my heartfelt indebtedness to my wife C.S. Nirmala Swamy and daughter S. Manjushri for their continuous assistance and cooperation extended throughout my research work.

—S. Srikanta Swamy

LIST OF TABLES

4.35 Source of variation, sum of squares, degrees of freedom, mean square, F value and significance of F regarding all the components of CTS (2 x 2 x 2 x 2 factorial design).

4.36 Source of variation, sum of squares, degrees of freedom, mean square, F value and significance of F regarding the achievement of physics.

4.37 Source of variation, sum of squares, degrees of freedom, mean square, F value and significance of F regarding the component determining the relevance of information (Programme of CTS) determining the credibility of a source.

4.38 Source of variation, sum of squares, degrees of freedom, mean square, F value and significance of F regarding the component determining the accuracy of the factual claim (Programme of CTS).

4.39 Source of variation, sum of squares, degrees of freedom, mean square, F value and significance of F regarding the component determining the credibility of a source (Programme of CTS).

4.40 Source of variation, sum of squares, degrees of freedom, mean square, F value and significance of F regarding the component identifying the unstated assumption (Programme of Critical thinking skills).

4.41 Source of variation, sum of squares, degrees of freedom, mean square, F value and significance of F regarding the component determining the strength of an argument (Programme of CTS).

4.42 Source of variation, sum of squares, degrees of freedom, mean square, F value and significance of F regarding the component distinguishing the statement of fact from value judgemt (Programme of CTS).

1

INTRODUCTION

Man is a rational animal, and ever since man came into existence he has been thinking. Man's interaction with the environment to fulfill his needs has resulted in the new discoveries and inventions. Though, every human being is capable of thinking, only a small percentage of them become great thinkers and their contributions are more in all walks of life. Scientists who have contributed wonderful gadgets, statesmen who have served the nation with good administration, novelists who have written great novels, poets who have composed outstanding poems, authors who have written original books and articles are all great thinkers. Although thinking is a natural function, the researches of Benjamin Bloom, and Arthur Whinbey have shown that, much of good thinking is not natural but acquired. Most of your day to day activities, such as decorating a room, opening of a lock when the key is lost, repairing of small gadgets, planning a trip do involve thinking. But this kind of thinking does not involve any regular pattern. Hence, by practicing the patterns of thinking it is possible to acquire higher level of thinking.

Meaning of Thinking

Many philosophers and psychologists have tried to define thinking in their own ways. In recent times, 'thinking' has been the concern of psychologists, researchers, and curriculum designers and even National Policy on Education (1986).

John Dewey defined thinking as "that operation in which present facts suggest other facts (or truths) in such a way as to induce belief in the latter upon the ground or warrant of the former."

According to Jepson, "thinking is essentially purposive directed and controlled at any rate in its earlier stages by the conscious exercise of will and set in motion by the conscious realization of the existence of a problem demanding solution."

Edward de Bono has done highly commendable work in the area of thinking through his Cognitive Research Trust (CoRT). It has developed a number of pedagogic theories wherein he has explained different strategies and tools for thinking. He also has defined thinking as "the processes of using one's brain to attempt to solve problem or to arrive at some conclusion."

All the above definitions convey the idea that thinking is a cognitive process used to manipulate information. Thinking also helps in solving problem, taking decisions, and in providing leadership in all walks of life and therefore, it is necessary to develop thinking abilities among the students by providing appropriate learning experience through effective classroom instruction.

Thinking and Instruction

The main task of teaching is not merely providing the information but to process it. In order to process the information, the teacher has to do a lot of thinking before transacting the information. Effective instruction, includes developing the cognitive abilities among the students and not simply passing on the information. The present instructional set up places memory at premium and thinking at a discount. Instruction helps in measuring the achievement of students understanding in subjects with reference to certain cognitive operations like memory, reasoning, identification and differentiation. This indicates that more emphasis in the classroom is for acquisition of knowledge and understanding. This inhibits students thinking effectively. Further, it has been the common observation of educationists that the thinking operations are rarely taught in the classroom. Most of the classroom teaching is limited in providing knowledge mechanically without giving scope for students effective participation in learning. As a result, learners' needs are neglected and hence there is a limited scope for developing cognitive abilities.

Therefore, there is a need to plan the classroom instructions in such a way that it should lead onto better cognitive behaviour, that help the teacher acquire the power to get knowledge. Cognitive abilities be developed including thinking abilities among students. A good teaching situation is one which helps in maximizing cognitive abilities. The task of students is not only to acquire various kinds of information found in educations curricula, but also to process the information which helps in achieving the objectives of Instructions. This implies good teaching ability on the part of the teacher to plan his lessons effectively and plan for development of higher mental ability especially thinking. Among other subjects of instructions, Science provides maximum scope for developing thinking ability.

Thinking and Science Instruction

Science is a body of systematic knowledge. Science is the investigation and interpretation of the natural phenomena which occurs in daily life. It is the inner desire of man which encourages him to find out the reasons for such happenings. The dynamic nature of science has resulted in giving rise to new branches of science like natural science, physical science and so on. Through physical science, it is possible to understand the laws and principles of natural phenomenon. In the area of physical science scientists have followed the process approach in understanding the natural phenomenon and to arrive at the new knowledge. The findings of the experiments are based on empirical data which lay emphasis on the objectivity of its approach, analysis and the generalization. All discoveries and inventions are due to the well-followed scientific steps and analysis. The discoveries and investigations done by the scientists involves various processes such as observation, classification, communication, formulation of hypotheses and experimentation. All this process involves various components of thinking skills.

Every individual interacts with the environment. All individual experience the laws and principles of nature. And hence, there is a need to make everyone understand the environment in which he lives. In addition to this, the new development of science and technology has brought about radical change in the society. This creates a need on the part of every individual to be more scientific in his approach. In this direction, school has a greater responsibility to play an active role. It is from this point of view, science education has to be strengthened.

The National Policy of Education (1986) emphasizes the role of science education in developing well defined abilities and values such as the spirit of inquiry, creativity, objectivity, the courage to question and an aesthetic sensibility. Further, the policy also insists on effective science education programme to make the learner to acquire problem solving and decision making skills and to discover the relationship with health, agriculture, industry and other aspects of daily life. In order to realize the goals of science education, the curriculum has also undergone lot of changes. As stated earlier, the present science curriculum focusses much on developing the cognitive abilities and skills. In this context, lot of studies have been conducted in the area of science curriculum. In the process of transacting the curriculum, different objectives are to be considered in science teaching. The following are the list of objectives for science teaching at the secondary level as envisaged in the National Policy of Education (1986). They are,

To:

— consolidate and strengthen knowledge, competencies and skills acquired at upper primary level acquire understanding of scientific concepts, principles and laws develop instrumental, communicational and problem-solving skills

— develop a scientific temper, scientific approach of scientific attitude such as open mindedness, intellectual honesty, courage to question and respect for human dignity and decision-making

— cultivate social, ethical, moral and aesthetic values which exalt and refine the life of the individual and society

— appreciate the contribution of scientists and develop sensitivity to possible uses of science and concern for clear environment and preservation of the ecosystem. Create an awareness of the need to guard against the possible misuse of science.

Therefore, the task of science teacher is to achieve the above mentioned objectives though learning experiences in the classroom. This implies a good exercise of thinking skills especially creative, analytical , and critical thinking. What is critical thinking? How is it related to science teaching? Let us discuss this in detail.

Critical Thinking Skills and Science Instruction

Effective teaching of science helps in developing abilities like reasoning, problem solving, arriving at generalization etc. Since these abilities vary from student to student, it is a general feeling that these abilities more or less individualistic and are very difficult to develop. But recently, Robert Ennis, David Krathwhole, de Bono and others believe that, the process of thinking is based on the subject matter and to develop proficiency in thinking through the subject involves a skill. Hence, thinking is more a skill than ability. By providing suitable examples and making an individual to practice, it is possible to improve one's thinking. The degree of improvement in thinking can also be assessed. Structured thinking process also involves the use of different thinking tools. Edward de Bono's CoRT programme insists on consistent use of the thinking tools such as P.M>I. (Plus, Minus, Interesting) A.G.O. (Aimsm, Goals, and Objectives) and C.A.F. (Consider All Factors). He has proved that thinking can be taught, like any other skill. The thinking tools used in the mental process can be defined, measured and improved upon, Hence thinking is considered as a skill (Franklin Institute Press 1979, National Education Association 1987, Freeman 1987 etc.)

Much thrust is being laid on developing thinking skills among students, since it helps them in taking proper decisions even in complex situations. There are quite a number of research findings indicating the novel and practical methods of teaching thinking skills, based on different components. The figure-1 indicates the different attributes of thinking skills.

Some of the companies of thinking skills are frequently seen in science teaching situations. There are many situations such as experimentation, problem solving and discovery involving such cognitive operations. If science teachers are convinced and trained about the various components of thinking skills then it is possible to develop some of these components deliberately. Even in the usual science teaching situations to some extent, attempts are being made by teachers to develop lower order thinking skills among students.

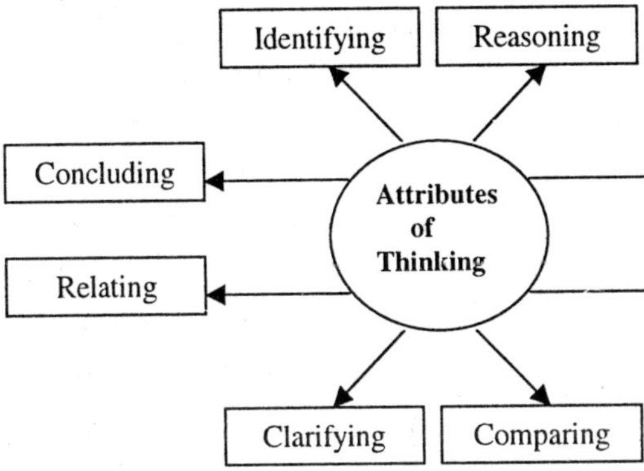

Figure 1. Attributes of Thinking

As discussed earlier, thinking involves many discrete operations. Of these, some of them are simple, and other are complex, depending upon the nature and purpose of specific operations involved. Thinking can be classified into reflective thinking, logical thinking, inductive thinking, creative thinking, clear thinking, practical thinking, productive thinking, lateral thinking, critical thinking and so on. The following figure indicates various types of thinking.

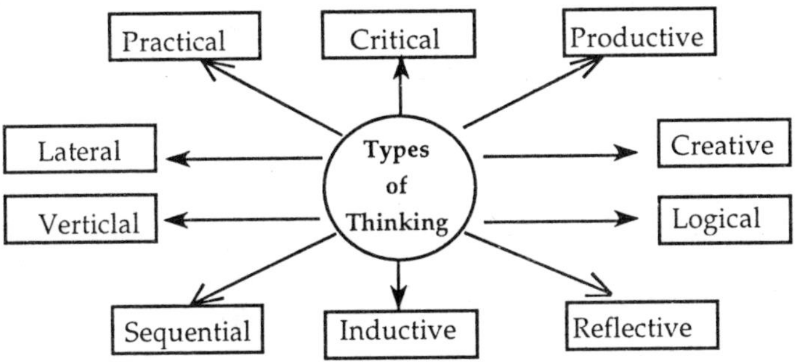

Figure 2. Types of Thinking

Though there are several types of thinking as explained by many Educationists and Psychologists (Dewey, Taba,

Burner, Asubel, Torrence, do Bono, Cornbleth, Dorothy, McClure, Edith West...), most of them are interested and slightly overlap with each other in some aspects of the congnitive process. Teaching of science involves different types of thinking depending upon the topics and the purpose with which it is being taught.

Creative thinking involves the invention of patterns, relationships, combinations, and products. Creative thinking is closely related to problem solving (as supported by J.R. Hayes). Creative thinking is largely a state of mind, which seems to be primarily guided and driven by a desire to seek the original. According to Parkin, *"creativity values mobility, reveals in exploration, it feels on flexibility and it honours diversity."* In addition to these types of thinking, there is one more type of thinking namely critical thinking which has not been identified by many experts as important as other thinking skills such as creative thinking. Some people have mistaken this type of thinking for fault finding or negative judgment. In fact, critical thinking consists essentially of judging the authenticity, worth or accuracy of information, a claim or assertion or a source of data. Clear knowledge and understanding of critical thinking will definitely help science teacher to acquaint its relationship with science teaching. Let us try to analyse some of the definitions of critical thinking.

According to Dewey, "Critical thinking involves active persistent and careful consideration of any belief or supposed form of knowledge in the light of the grounds that support it and further conclusions to which it tends."

Catherin Cornbleth, has described critical thinking based on the following points.

"Critical thinking is not inherently negative. Skepticism is not synonymous with negativism. It means questioning what might otherwise be taken for granted or summarily rejected. Critical thinking can lead to affirmation on former grounds as well as to debunking and modification or rejection of idea. Critical thinking has both conservative and liberating potential. Skepticism does not mean automatically questioning anything and everything."

According to Robert Ennis, Critical thinking is reasonable reflective thinking that is focused on deciding what to believe or do.

From the above definitions one can understand that critical thinking involves careful consideration of a given situation in terms of all the information so as to evaluate or to arrive at appropriate generalization based on certain criteria.

Research in education directed towards thinking has been the concern of recent psychologists and educationists. There have been a number of efforts aimed at teaching of thinking in general and different types of thinking in particular. Though efforts in the field of education concerned with teaching of critical thinking have generally used a hasty conception of what is involved in judging statements. Efforts done by Anderson and Smith, Drussel and Maychow, Whood Conant, have yielded only a smaller degree of desirable result. There were also attempts to develop programmes for improving the conceptual clarity regarding critical thinking. This includes different objectives such as

TO:

- examine the literature on the goals of the schools and the literature on the criteria of good thinking.
- select from this literature those aspects which come under the following basic notion of critical thinking as the correct assessing of the statements.
- elaborate the criteria to apply in making such assessments to the extent that there are criteria.

— simplify rather than elaborate the result by classifying some aspects under others that are logically more basic.

— simplify further by logically analyzing them into basic factors or dimensions or critical thinking.

The above mentioned objectives will be of greater help for any researcher who undertakes the development of the programme of critical thinking skills. Robert Ennis who has done a commendable work in the field of thinking skills has suggested various aspects which are to be considered while developing the programme on critical thinking skills. They are, grasping the meaning of a statement, judging various aspects such as the problem identification, assumption, adequacy of the definition, authenticity of the source, reliability of the statement, applicability of the principle, specificity of the statement etc. In addition to the above aspects of critical thinking, there are three important dimensions namely; logical dimension (refers to judging of alleged relationships, meanings of words and statement), critical dimension (covers the knowledge of the criteria for judging statements), and pragmatic dimension (taking of decision as to the whether the statement is good enough) for the purpose or not.

Recently, much attention and interest is shown for the assessment and development of critical thinking skills. in this consideration, quite a number of researches have been done on this area. The contemporary writings about critical thinking can be classified into three categories namely;

Writings concerened with conceptualising, defining and measuring critical thinking (writings of Ennis 1962, 1981, 1985).

Studies directed toward the development, implementation and evaluation of instructoin of programme, that teach thinking (Covington 1985, de Bono's CoRT programme).

Writings which include details regarding criteria which are to be considered while evaluating the different programmes on thinking. (Storn Bergs 1983).

Thus teaching or critical thinking involves a set of intellectual tasks, thinking dimensions and also the use of the higher mental operations.

Components of Critical Thinking Skills

Use of critical thinking skills do not mean drawing favourable judgment, but encouragement a person to think deeply, to seek clarification or understand objects. Further, critical thinking involves a collection of thinking operations, which help a person to determine the merits and demerits of an object. There are several components which decide the operations of critical thinking skills. There are several attributes which decides the nature of critical thinking skills. The following figure indicates the attributes of Critical Thinking skills.

The following are the essential components of critical thinking skills. (Terry Applogate and Anitha Harnadek).

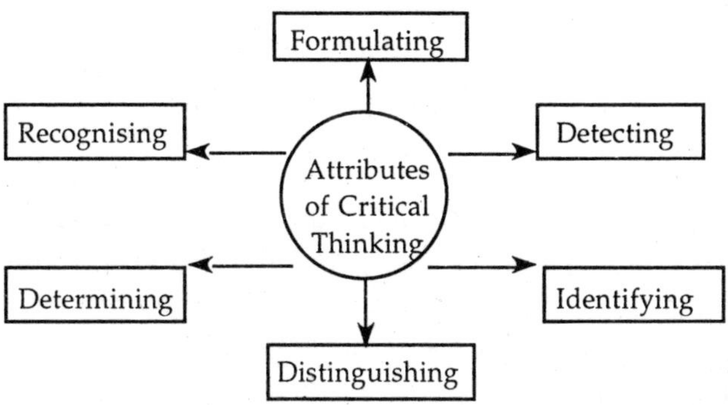

Figure 3. Attributes of Critical Thinking

1. Distinguishing between statements of verifiable facts and value claims.

2. Distinguishing relevant from irrelevant information, claims or reasons.
3. Determining the factual accuracy of a statement.
4. Dete. mining the credibility of a written source.
5. Identifying the ambiguous claims or arguments.
6. Identifying the unstated assumptions.
7. Detecting bias.
8. Identifying logical fallacies.
9. Recognizing the logical inconsistencies in a line of reasoning.
10. Determining the strength of an argument or claim.

Each of the above components of critical thinking skills consist of specific procedure and a set of operating rules. These components indicate the possibility that, science also provides situations to test such components of critical thinking skills. Though direct studies have been made to process the mental operations of students to develop thinking skill, using problem solving techniques. Although the attempts have not been made in the direction of critical thinking, Joyce and Weil have discussed a number of information processing models such as concept attainment, inductive thinking, inquiry training, cognitive growth models etc. These information processing models are very useful to begin any training of subject matter for class room teachers. They also help teachers to know how students think, and the different techniques useful in processing thinking ability (Jerome Bruner, Hilda Taba, David Ausubel, Richard Suckman...). Based on these models, studies also have been taken up in India (D'Lima and others).

These models are also useful in planing variety of teaching strategies to improves the students' abilities to process the information. Further, the teaching-learning situation will be effective science participation. At the school level lot of emphasis has been laid regarding effective science teaching. In order to make teaching effective, the different approaches, methods and modes of teaching will be of greater importance. As a result of this, students will be made to be alternative regarding the learning of the subject matter rather than improving the knowledge. Apart from this, teaching of science at the secondary school also involves number of tasks on the part of the teacher. Some of these tasks include selection of supplementary information from various sources, judging the suitability of an approach or a method to teach a topic, possibility of applying a given theory or a principle in a novel situation etc, involves critical thinking. In addition to this, there are other tasks related to practical aspect of science teaching such as, selection of suitable apparatus for an experiment, judging the suitability of topics for demonstrations, identification of assumptions in an experimental set up, identification of verifiable facts etc. also involves components of critical thinking. In fact, contributions made by great scientists, are due to critical analysis of phenomenon without which it would have been very difficult to think of devising gadgets instruments that are practicable.

Therefore, it is very essential to develop critical thinking skills among science teachers who in turn help in improving quality of science education.

Need for the Study

Teaching of science at the school level has as already discussed has taken the shape of merely telling and sometimes demonstrating experiments. The higher cognitive abilities like suspended judgment, open mindedness, establishing cause and effect relationships, problem solving, creative and critical thinking are not given enough emphasis in science teaching. Science, compared to other school subjects lends itself to better and deeper analysis of the physical phenomenon around us. It is here the human individual can exercise his mental powers not only in understanding science but discovering new things in science. It is possible to look at several physical laws not only from one point of view of generalistic but through critical analysis and suggest alternatives. It is high time that science teachers realize and teach science for achieving these higher objectives of helping learners to become more competent students of science. The National Policy of Education (1986) has rightly emphasized the quality improvement in teaching as well as development of abilities to learn. Science especially physical science requires lot of thinkers. Thinkers who could critically examine phenomenon and suggest alternatives by properly relating several of the phenomenal variables. Such thinking that helps them differentiate better, judge better and suggest alternatives. The duty and task of a science teacher in general and physics teacher in particular should be to improve such thinking skills among their students so that understanding concepts would become easy and better achievement and generation of new ideas could also be the outcome.

In India, several attempts have been made in this direction and there are several significant research studies conducted which have surfaced the feasibility of several approaches to science teaching. Some of them are on Inquiry training, synectic approaches and so on. Critical examining the curriculum at the school level as such that suggestions for teaching them to achieve better goals are also attempted by Vardhini physical and biological science at school level. But many of these studies are either supporting the methodology or improvement in achievement. There are very few studies where the learner abilities are focused.

More so, the pre-service teachers who are the future ring masters of the classroom, have not been the target of research in terms of improving cognitive abilities like thinking or critical thinking. If science teacher who are practitioners improve or get trained in these thinking skills, they are sure to be successful in imparting quality education in schools. When can this happen? Surely, at the teacher training level. If the trainees of teaching science are thoroughly trained to think in any one of the types, then, in turn they may transfer this to their students.

This logic has been attempted to be applied in physical science for students who are undergoing training programme. Thinking especially critical thinking is a trainable skill. There are several studies conducted abroad that gives hints regarding the development of the skill. Therefore, it is worthwhile venturing to take up impact studies on teacher trainees in a thorough manner in one of the science subjects namely methods of teaching physics to develop the programme to improve their critical thinking skills.

Scope of the Study

Teachers training course being a professional course involves training of lot of competencies and skills on the part of the teacher trainees. There are different areas such as practice teaching, preparation of teaching aids (Audio-Visual aids) preparation of unit test etc. which involves lot of cognitive skills. These skills will help the teacher trainees in selection of the content areas, organising the content material, construction of test items etc. Even the planning of lessons involve selection of the content, content analysis, writing of instructional objectives, designing of learning exp etc. Higher level of cognitive skills will definitely help teacher to plan and teach lessons effectively.

In addition to the above practical aspects, the teacher trainees are expected to be thorough with the methods of teaching the special subjects along with other subjects. Under the methods of teaching, the trainees will come across different approaches and methods of teaching knowledge of audio-visual aids, and also planning of the content in relation to the suitability of methods and approaches. Critical thinking skills being the cognitive skills may help the teacher trainees to a great extent in the above mentioned areas.

In the present study, the researcher has used several approaches and strategies to find out whether there would be any method to improve the initial level of critical thinking skills among the trainees and in turn how far these skills may help in influencing the performance of trainees who have taken methods of teaching physics on their own specialization.

Hence, the scope of the present study is restricted to measure the initial level of critical thinking skills through the administering of Tools of Critical Thinking Skills (TOCTS) and later providing them with Programme of Critical Thinking Skills (POCTS). Further, asertaining the change on the significant difference between initial level and final level of critical thinking skills through the use of post test. If there is a difference between initial level and final level of critical thinking skills, which are attributed to the effectiveness of the programme. In addition to this, scope of the study is also extended to find the influence of variables like sex, intelligence and S.E.S. on critical thinking skills.

In the later stage of the study, the impact of the programme of critical thinking skills on the achievement of the trainees in methods of teaching physics will be also studied.

Statement of the Problem

"An impact of a programme of critical thinking skills on the achievement of secondary school teacher trainees of Bangalore city."

Objectives of the Research

1. To develop a tool to measure critical thinking skills among the Secondary School Teacher Trainees of Bangalore City.
2. To develop a programme of critical thinking skills based on methods of teaching Physics.
3. To study the impact of the programme of critical thinking skills on the achievement of Secondary School Teacher Trainees, in methods of teaching Physics.
4. To find out the interaction of Sex, Intelligence, S.E.S. and critical thinking skills on the achievement of Secondary School Teacher Trainees, in methods of teaching Physics.

Overview of the Study

The nature of the study, need for the study and objectives of the study, and statement of the problem have been discussed in this chapter.

In the next chapter relevant studies which are related to the area of the present study, under the chapter entitled "Review of Related Literature" will be discussed.

The third chapter deals with the methodology and procedures used in the study. It includes the description of the variables, sampling technique, tools used in the study and other related points. The development of the programme of critical thinking skills is also discussed in detail.

The fourth chapter deals with the analysis and interpretations of the data.

Lastly, the fifth chapter contains summary and conclusions concerned with the present study.

2

REVIEW OF RELATED LITERATURE

In the previous chapter the importance, the need for the study and the statement of problem have been dealt with. In this chapter, a brief review of studies done in the present area is made. To understand the reason for giving the review of related literature, it would be worthwhile to note its importance. It serves a variety of purposes. It assumes familiarity with both previous theory and research to the researcher. It helps in many ways such as to have conceptual frame of reference for the contemplated research, clues regarding the research design, methodology and the tools to be used to analyse the data. Hence, it becomes imperative on the part of the researcher to review some of the work done, by other researchers. The researcher has reviewed number of studies done in India and other countries to trace out the development of cognitive studies. The right literature obtained in connection with the present study is more from other countries than in India. Though in India, many studies seems to have not been done exclusively in the area of critical thinking, but studies have been done in the area of cognitive processing, cognitive abilities, critical thinking, abstract reasoning, critical analysis, problem solving, evaluation of curriculum etc.

In other countries, sincere attempts were made to study the cognitive abilities as early as 1928 when Prath has reviewed

142 experimental studies. Out of this, nearly 46 references were identified related to thinking. There were also studies conducted by creative thinking, problem solving etc. (Normal Majer, Bruner Torrance Gagne, Piaget, McHonry, McCurtly, Rozer, Saljo...). From 1960 onwards, innumerable studies have been conducted in the area of cognitive processing in the name of various type of cognitive skills.

Studies Conducted in India

a) Studies Related to Area of Cognitive Abilities and Development

Cognitive Abilities

Sandeep, P., (1979) has conducted a study on "Classroom Interaction and Cognitive Development in Primary School Children" at Osmania University.

The major objectives of the investigation were: (i) to ascertain the level of cognitive development in primary school children, (ii) to ascertain how schools differed in the classroom interaction on the cognitive development of children. The following hypotheses were framed and tested: (i) if perceptual activities were the bases for the later emerging intellectual operations then there would be an inter-association between reorganization, schematization and topological, protective and Euclidean space dimensions. (ii) If concept attainment followed a sequence from the concrete to the abstract, the qualitative topological features emerged earlier than metrical protective and Euclidean space. (iii) If culture to which the children belonged had a say in the development of concepts, then Indian children and they should vary in the attainment of these abilities. (iv) Within the Indian culture, if the Indian setting was homogeneous without religious, caste and income influences, then there would not be any differences among the school-going children in the attainment of the cognitive concepts.

The sample consisted of primary school-going children of government schools, private schools, aided schools, central schools, private schools of Hyderabad and Ranga Reddy district. The children were drawn from Grades IV and V and a small number of children from Grade I were taken from comparison purposes. The instruments used were Typology of Teaching Styles and Bennet and Jords, Picture Ambiguity Test and Picture Integration Test of David Elkind and others, and Special Orientation Tasks of Piaget and Inhelder. Factor analysis was used to analyze the data.

Following were the major findings: (i) Various activities and orientations associated with perceptual activities and special orientation were independent of each other. (ii) Children at lower ages were familiar with topological space operation and with increase in age acquired the next operations, projective and Euclidean. (iii) Age was related to increase in perceptual activities and cognitive operations were found to be based on their respective background like sex, religion, caste, income, parents' education, occupation and leisure activity. (v) Schools differed in their classroom interaction which affected adversely the attainment of perceptual and cognitive skills.

Bansal, I.K. (1979) has conducted a research on *"A comparative study of the abilities of students of modern and traditional mathematics."*

The objectives of the study were to find out whether the school students studying modern mathematics at the secondary level possessed more critical thinking abilities than those studying traditional mathematics at the level (ii) to find out the factor patterns of the abilities of students studying modern mathematics as well as students studying traditional mathematics at the secondary schools level. (iv) To compare the factor patterns of the abilities of students studying modern mathematics with those studying traditional mathematics.

The sample consisted of 424 and 404 students from Delhi. The tests of critical and creative thinking were conducted along with the other tests. Statistical techniques like mean, median, standard deviation, quartile deviation, factor analysis, and product moment correlation techniques were used. The major finding of the study were:

1. Students of modern mathematics possessed more critical thinking than those studying traditional mathematics cirruculum.
2. Results obtained by orthogonal rotation were (a) critical thinking ability as well as other variables of critical thinking namely, number serves number classification inference and symbol manipulation and moderate loadings on the factor of hypothesis verification for both the samples. The remaining variable of critical thinking and moderate loading on the factor of hypothesis verifications for the students of modern mathematics only (b) critical thinking abilities as well as other variables of critical thinking namely last letters, utility text, number combinations and make up problems had moderate grading on different thinking for both the samples.

Joseph T.T. (1979) has conducted as research on *"A study of some predictors of achievement in chemistry at the pre degree level."*

The objectives of the study were to find out the Association between each of the independent Variables and different achievement levels in chemistry (high, average, and low achiever) in terms of ability of each of the Independent variables to demonstrate between the different achievement levels compared in pairs to find out the degree of association between each of the Independent variables and achievement in chemistry to develop an equation (or equation) to predict achievement in chemistry using efficient predictors identified and to obtain factor instructed in terms of the variables for two extreme achievement levels in chemistry the study was conducted on a representative sample of 500 pre – degree students of Kerala. Critical thinking was considered as one of the variables somnd the ten variables selected (one dependent and nine Independent) the data was analyzed using product moment so efficient of correlation, multiple prediction equations and factor analysis.

The major findings were:

1. All the nine independent variables correlated significantly with achievement in chemistry at the pre – degree level.
2. All the nine Independent variables disseminated between the high achievers and the average achievers and low achievers. This implies that critical thinking is significantly related to achievement in science. Further, critical thinking discriminates between high average and low achievers.

Pushpa Vathamma, Y., (1980) has conducted a study on *"Impact of Social primary Deprivation on Cognitive Styles of Primary School Children"* at Osmania University.

The major objectives of the study were: (I) to ascertain the cognitive styles of primary school children, (ii) to assess the level of cognitive abilities, and (iii) to find out the impact of school deprivation on the cognitive styles and abilities of primary school children.

Variable taken for study were biological variables, school variables, social variables parental variables and deprivation index. The sample consisted on 265 boys and girls in the age range of 5+ to 13+ from Grades I, III, V from eight schools under different types of management, representing schools from semiurban, rural, and urban areas of a tribal region of Andhra Pradesh. The instruments used were an adapted version of Prolonged Deprivation Scale developed by Tripathy and Mishra, Draw-a-Person Test, Children's Embedded Figure Test, Picture Complection Test, Koh's Blocks, object Asembly, Lorge-Thorndike Test-I and Lorge-Thorndike Test-II. The investigator administered the test individually and collected the data. Factor analysis and multiple regression analyzing were used to analyse the data.

Important findings of the study were: (I) Residential accommodation, home environment, economic sufficiency, food, clothing, parental characteristics, interaction with parents and recreational experiences were found to be the most significant factors of each of which would make a child socially deprived. Incidentally, it was also found that school, father's education, and income were highly related to the above factors. (ii) The children of high school-educated fathers were experiencing higher deprivation in residential accommodation while the children of illiterate fathers were highly deprived and those of college-educated fathers were least deprived. (iv) The children of illiterate fatehers were more deprived in income sufficiency and the children of college-educated fathers were least deprived in this regard. (v) In food and clothing conditions, the children of middle school-educated fathers were more deprived and the children of college-educated fathers were least deprived. (vi) In parental characteristics and interaction with parents, the children of illiterate fathers were experiencing higher deprivation and those of college-educated fathers were least deprived. (vii) In recreational experiences, the children of college-educated fathers were more deprived and the children of middle-school-educated fathers were less deprived. (viii) Children were less field independent at the early ages and it gradually increased with age. (ix) The children of Grade I were highly field dependent and the children of Grade II were more field dependent than those of Grade V. (x) The tribal private, and semi-urban school children were more field independent. The aided school children were lease field independent, and the government school children and the rural children did not sow a significant difference whether they were less field independent than the tribal, semi-urban and private school children. (xi) The children of professionals, semi-skilled workers and business people were highly field independent. The children of manual labour and clerks were less field independent than those of executives and the unemployed. (xii) The children of Hindu religion were more field independent than Muslims and Christians. (xii) There were no differences among boys and girls in their field independence.

Ray P., (1952) has conducted a study on the "*Effects of Attribution Training on the Development of Intellectual Achievement, Responsibility and Cognitive Performance among Lower Class Children.*"

The objectives of the study were (i) to measure intellectual achievement responsibility of low income group elementary school children reading in classes III, IV, (ii) to introduce an intervention programme at four different states which were equally spaced in terms of time, and (iii) to observe if changes in the attribution process has significant relationship with mental abilities and cognitive competence as revealed by academic achievement and other related attributional process.

Two hundred students (100 boy and 100 girls) of three elementary schools of Cuttack coming from families of poor socio-economic homes were randomly assigned to experimental and control groups. The instruments used were Crandill's IAR Scales, Bialers I.E Locus of Control Scale,

Robinson's n-Ach Questionnaire, Raven's Progressive Matrices, Peirs-Harries Self-concept Questionnaire, and school achievement test. Training was phased into four stages through 15 lectures, goat-setting through training programme was composite but the post-tests were taken in between to observe systematic change, if any, depending on training, using an additive model. Data obtained were analyzed by using chi-square and analysis of variance.

The major findings were: (I) Intervention programmes produced significant changes in IAR, IAR (failure), related attributional processes (self-esteem, I-E control, n-Ach), mental ability and school achievement. (ii) There was significant variation in attributional process scores, mental ability and achievement from phase-I of the post-test through phase-4 with the only exception of self-esteem. (iii) There were significant interactions between treatment and post-test sessions on each of the variables. At each of the post-tests the experimental group of children had higher scores than the control group children. (iv) Changes in IAR (total) were related to IAR (success), IAR (failure) and school achievement for both the groups. (v) IAR (failure was not related to any of the variables included in the study for both the groups. (v) IAR (failure was not related to any of the variables included in the study for both the groups. I-E control was positively related to self-concept scores of the experiment group children and negatively related to school achievement. (vi) Self-concept was significantly related to mental ability, n-Ach and school achievement. n-Ach was only moderately related to mental ability and achievement and the relationship between mental ability and achievement was positive in all case.

Chaudhary, G.G., (1983) has conducted a study *"An Investigation into the Trends of Creative Thinking Ability of Pupils of Age Group 11+ to 13+ in relation to Some Psycho-socio Correlates"* at S.P. University

The objective of the study were, (i) to prepare a reliable and valid creative thinking ability test, (ii) to study the trend of critical thinking ability of pupils of different areas, (iii) to study the trend of critical thinking ability of pupils of different sexes, (iv) to study to trend of creative thinking ability of pupils of age group 11 to 13, and (v) to study the trend of creative thinking ability of pupils in relation to their socio-economic status (SEC), need achievement (n-Ach), IQ parental behaviour, anxiety, security-insecurity feelings, radicalism vital vs. conservation, flexibility vs. rigidity, suggestivity and emotional stability.

The Creative Thinking Ability Test was standardized on a sample of 1000 pupils of which 394 were from urban area and 606 were from rural area. The reliability and validity of the test were established. The percentiles and percentile rank norms were established for different age groups. For measuring socio-economic states (SES), n-Ach, IQ, anxiety, security-insecurity, and personality traits, inventories were used. All these tools were standardized by different persons. Factorial design was used tostudy creative thinking ability in relation to various psycho-socio variables.

The major findings were: 1. There was no significant difference between the mean creative thinking scores of male and female children of rural and urban areas. 2. There was a marked difference between the mean scores on the test of children of three age groups. 3. The hight the socio-economic status, the higher was the creative thinking ability of the student. 4. The higher the n-Ach, the higher was the creative thinking ability of the student. 5. The students with high IQ did not have more creative thinking ability than the students of the low IQ. 6. The students belonging to the high parental behaviour group did not have more creative thinking ability than the students belonging to the low parental behaviour groups. 7. The students with low anxiety had more creative thinking ability than students with high anxiety. 8. The higher the security, the higher was the creative thinking ability. 9. The higher the radicalism trait, the higher was the creative thinking ability of the students. 10. Students with the flexibility trait had more creative thinking ability than students with the rigidity trait. 11. The students with low suggestibility had more creative thinking ability than the students with high suggestibility. 12. The students with high emotional stability had more creative thinking ability than the students with low emotional stability.

Deshpande, M.B., (1984) has conducted a study on *"An Analytical Study of Cognitive-Affective Development and Scholastic Achievement of Tribal Secondary School Student"* at Nagpur University.

The study aimed at critically examining the achievement, the intellectual and affective development of tribal students, especially in comparison with non- tribal students. Hypotheses were formulated under three heads (i) the study of cognitive abilities, (ii) the study of personality make-ups and (iii) scholastic achievement.

The sample for the study was drawn from the tribals and non-tribals of the Chhatisgarh region of Madhya Pradesh. The tools used for the collection of data were: (i) General Intelligence Test, (ii) Numerical Ability Test, (iii) Verbal Ability Test, (vi) Reasoning Test, (v) Bernreuter Personality Inventory, (vi) Scholastic Achievement Test.

The following were some of the major findings: 1. Mean scores of non-tribal students were significantly higher than those of the tribal students on all the cognitive tests. 2. Mean scores of the non-tribal boys and non-tribal girls were significantly higher than those of tribal boys and tribal girls on all cognitive tests. 3. Urban tribal boys and urban tribal girls were sufficiently higher than rural tribal boys and rural tribal girls. 4. Gond tribal students were better than those of all other castes on all cognitive tests. 5. Bariya and Khadia castes students were lowest in performance. 6. Tribal students scored lower than non-tribal students on Bernreuter Personality Inventory which indicated that tribal students were more emotionally stable and more social than non-tribal students. 7. Tribal students scored more than non-tribal students on an attitude scale which indicated a more favourable attitude of tribal students than non-tribal students toward education. 8. Tribal girls were found more social, stable and emotionally well developed than non-tribal girls. 9. Tribal girls had a more favourable attitude than non-tribal girls towards schooling. 10. Rural tribal boys and girls were emotionally better developed and more social than urban boys and girls. 11. Rural tribal boys and girls had a more favourable attitude than urban tribal boys and girls. 12. Tribal students were more educationally backward than non-tribal students.

Das, P., (1985) has conducted a study on the "*Structure of Cognitive Abilities among National and Tribal Children as a Function of Developmental Level.*"

The objectives of the study were (i) to measure different information processing abilities of children,(ii) to make a comparative analysis of processing habits using the subcultural groups as independent variables and each of the measures as a dependent variable, (iii) to find out whether there was any interactive relationship between the organismic variables (age, social groups)and the process variables, and (iv) to analyze the structure of cognitive abilities in the case of different subgroups of normal and tribal children of 7 to 10 years of age. The hypotheses of the study were: (i) There will be significant differences among children varying in age and social background for each of the measures on cognitive abilities. (ii) there will be a significant interactive relationship between age and social background with regard to various processing variables. (iii) the structure of cognitive abilities will be different for children varying in age and social background.

One hundred and fifty boys were selected from classes I and V equally drawn from normal and tribal schools of Puri and Keonijhar districts of Orissa state. Twenty five high – SES and 25 low – SES children under each group served as the subjects of the present study. Twenty-five boys of classes I and V selected from three tribal schools of Keonijhar district formed the sample of tribal students. The normal children were divided in to groups, namely high –SES and low – SES. Students were classified under two age-groups, viz. those below seven years age and those above ten years age. The tools employed for the studywere Figure Copying Test (FCT), Hidden Patterns Test (HPT), Raven's Coloured Progressive Matrices (RPM), Visual Short Term Memory (VSTM), Digit Span Forward and Backward (DSF, DSB), Memory-for-Designs (MFD), Children's Embedded Figures Test (CEFT), Matching Familiar Figures Test (MFFT), Colour Naming and Colour Word Test (C, CW) and Culture Fair Intelligence test (CFIT). The average time taken to administer all the tests on a single child was 2.5 hours. The data were analyzing using 2-3 factorial analysis of variance. The intercorrelations of all test scores for different sub-groups were computed using the varimax rotation factor analysis technique.

The findings of the study were: (i) Children above ten years were superior to children under seven years in analytical ability. (ii) Children coming from high –SES background were significantly superior to those from low –SES normal and tribal children. (iii) The performance of low –SES normal children was very close to that of tribal children at both age levels. (iv) Younger children were less intelligent than older ones. (v) High – SES normal children performed much better than low –SES normal and tribal children in both the immediately memory abilities at both age levels. (vi) The span of attention and memory of low –SES and normal and tribal children were very short compared to those of high – SES normal children. (vii) High –SES normal children committed less error comared to low –SES normal and tribal children at both age levels. (ix) The younger children took more time and committed more errors than other older children. (x) The tribal children took more time and committed more errors than low –SES normal children who were inferior to high –SES normal children in the C, CW test. (xi) The low –SES normal and tribal children were poor in the perceptual ability and had more interference effect than thehigh –SES normal children. (xii) For the younger age groups of children. FCT, RPM, VSTM, DSB, CEFT, MEFT, and CFIT were located with more than one factor and were considered as mixed tests. (xiii) For children in the above-ten-age-group, it was found that children adopted more simultaneous processing habits as reflected by FCT, HPT, RPM, CEFT, and CFIT. (iv) Students who were highly as well as lowly motivated towards students activities scored significantly higher than the moderately motivated on the 'Sober-Happy-go-lucky' trait. (v) There was no significant difference among students who were highly, moderately and lowly motivated towards student activities on the Phlegnatic-Excitable, Obedient-Assertive, Expedient- Conscientious, Tough-minded-Tender-minded, Placid-Apprehensive, Group-dependent-Self-sufficient, Undisciplined-Self-Conflict-Controlled, and Relaxed-Tense traits.

Deo, B., (1985) has conducted a study on the *"Cognitive Style and Cognitive Ability of Tribal and Non-Tribal School Pupils."*

The objectives of the investigations were (i) to study the cultural differences in the cognitive styles of tribal and non-tribal high school students (ii) to study the cultural differences in the general intelligence of tribal and non-tribal high school students, and (iii) to study the cultural differences in the creative thinking of tribal and non-tribal students.

The samples for the study were drawn from high school students of Ranchi. The tribal group of 160 students consisted of the male, female, Christian, Sarns, Oraon and Munds students of the age-group 12-14 years. The Non-tribal group of 80 students consisted of male and female Hindu students divided into high-caste and scheduled-caste. The data were collected with the help of Wilkin's Embedded Figure test (EPT). Raven's Progressive Matrices, and Mehdi's Non-verbal Creative Thinking Test. The obtained scores were treated statistically using two non-parametric techniques.

The major findings of the study were: (i) Tribals were more oriented toward field dependence and towards field independence than the non-tribals. (ii) The scores, when tested in the context of the various sub-groups based on ethnic, religious, sex and caste factors, failed to show any consistent trends. One consistency, however, was that the high-caste ones. (iii) Male and female tribal and non-tribal students differed in field dependence, whereas this difference was not noticed in case of field independence. (iv) As regards creative thinking, the results obtained showed that the tribal and non-tribal students did not differ among themselves. Similar results were obtained for the difference sub-groups. A highly significant association among the three variables in case of tribal students and non-tribal students was found. (v) cognitive style was found to be associated with academic achievement.

Creative Thinking

Desai, N.N., (1987) has conducted a study on *"An Investigation into the Creative Thinking ability of Students of Higher Secondary of Gujarat State in the Context of some Psycho-socia Factors"* at SP University.

The objectives of the study were, (i) to prepare a reliable and valid creative thinking ability test, (ii) to study the trend of creative thinking ability of pupils of higher secondary schools, (iii) to study the trends of creative thinking ability of pupils of different sexes, (iv) to study the trends of creative thinking ability of pupils of science and common streams, (v) to study the creative thinking ability of pupils of different socio-economic levels, and (vi) to study creative thinking ability in relation to scholastic achievement, anxiety and reasoning ability.

A verbal and non-verbal creative thinking ability test was constructed to measure fluency, flexibility, and originality (by verbal test) and fluency, flexibility and elaboration by a non-verbal test. The test was standardized over a sample of 608 students which included students from rural and urban areas, both girls and boys. The reliability of the test was established by test-retest, split-half, Rulon Formula and Flanagan Formula. It managed from 0.82 to 0.90. The concurrent and congruent validity were established. The SES scale by B.V. Patel and I.A. Vora, the Anxiety Scale by Nijhawan, the Non-verbal Reasoning Test by the investigator, the percentage marks obtained by the students at the SSC Examination were used for the study. For studying questionaire. The 2 x 2 factorial design was adopted and analysis of variance technique was used for testing the hypotheses.

The major findings were: 1. There was no difference in creative thinking ability of urban and rural higher secondary students. 2. There were no sex differences with regard to creative thinking ability of higher secondary students. 3. There was no difference between the means of high SES and low SES students. 4. There was no significant difference between the means of high SES and low SES students. 5. The mean difference between two groups, namely, the high anxiety and low anxiety group, was highly significant and was in favour of the low anxiety group. 6. The students with the radical personality trait were more creative. 7. The students with a low neuroticism level were more creative. 8. The students with high emotional stability were better in creative thinking than students with a low emotional stability. 9. The students with good reasoning ability were better in creative thinking than students with poor reasoning ability. 10. The students with higher scholastic achievement were found better in creative thinking than students with low scholastic achievement.

Patel, J.Z., (1987) has conducted a study on *"An Investigation into the Effectiveness of the Purdue Creative Thinking Programme on the Creative Abilities of Elementary School Children"* at SP University.

The objectives of the study were: (i) to provide standard creative thinking programmes in Gujarati for elementary school children, (ii) to study the effect of the programmes on the creative level of the children, (iii) to study the effect of the programmes on the creativity components, viz., fluency, flexibility, and originality, (iv) to verify whether the main effect of IQ was significant, (v) to investigate the main effect of sex, and (vi) to study whether there exists any interaction effect on the creativity and its component measures.

The eight classes of different schools selected from Kheda districk were equated on the basis of the scores made by the students on creative ability test prepared and standardized by J.Z. Patel. The creative thinking programme was translated into Gujarati. Out of 32 programmes, 18 were translated into Gujarati. Some other similar programmes were prepared by the ivestigator. The Intelligence Test prepared by J.Z. Patel was also administered to students of eight classes. Out of the eight classes, four were treated as experimental classes where the programmes were implemented. The remaining four classes were treated as control classes. The 2 x 2 x 2 factorial design was used. (Treatment x IQ x Sex) and the analysis of variance was used to analyse the performance of the students.

The major findings were: 1. The main effect of training given to the experimental group was significant for creativity and its two components measures, viz., fluency and originality. 2. The research confirmed the effectiveness of creative thinking training in the Indian setting. In spite of big classes, rigid classroom control, memorization and respect for teachers in comparison with American classes, the gain in creative thinking ability was noteworthy. 3. The main effect of IQ was significant but sex was not significant. The minimum IQ played an important role in the development of creativity of a child. There was no significant interaction effect on creativity and its components. 4. The creativity training could be practically imparted to the children in a developing country like India.

Piyavadee Boonsathron, (1988) has conducted a study on *"Creative Thinking Ability of Students of Higher Secondary Schools of Bangkok in the Context of Some Psycho-Social Factors"* at SP University.

The objectives of the study were: (i) to prepare a creative thinking ability test, (ii) to study the main effects of sex, grade and socio-economic status on the students, and (iii) to study creative thinking ability (CTA) in relation to students' adjustment, anxiety, neuroticism, radicalism and students' self-done activities.

The investigator constructed and standardized a creative thinking ability test over a sample of 543 students of class X and XI of Bangkok. The reliability coefficients established by the test- retest method, splif-half method, Rulon Formula and Flanagan formula were 0.79, 0.80, 0.82 and 0.78 respectively. Percentile norms were established for classes X and XI. Other tools used for collecting data were, (I) the

Adjustment Problem Inventory by J.C. Parikh and M.T. Patel, (ii) the Test Anxiety Scale of Children by H.K. Nijhawan, (iii) the Neuroticism Scale and Radicalism vital signs Conventionalism Scale by A.S. Patel, (iv) the Self Done Activities Scale by I.A. Vora, and(v) the Socio-Economic Scale by B.V. Patel and I.A. Vora. The 2 x 2 fraction design was adopted to study the effect of independent variables.

The major findings were:

1. There was no significant difference between the mean performance of boys and girls included in the sample.
2. There was no difference in creative thinking ability between students coming from high SES and low SES.
3. The students of grade XI had higher creative thinking ability than those of grade X.
4. The students with high adjustment level were superior to students with low adjustment level on creative thinking ability.
5. The students of grade XI and grade X were almost the same as far as creative thinking ability was concerned. The interaction effect of adjustment effect of adjustment and grade was highly significant.
6. The students with low anxiety level and higher creative thinking ability than students with high anxiety level. The students of grade XI were superior in creative thinking ability to students of class X. The interaction effect of grade and anxiety was significant.
7. Students having a low neuroticism lever were more creative than students with a high neuroticism

level. The interaction effect between grade and neuroticism was significant.

8. The students of the high radicalism group and low radicalism group were almost the same as far as creative thinking ability was concerned. The interaction effect between grade and radicalism was not significant.
9. The students having high self-done activity level and more creative thinking ability than students having low self-done activity leer. The interaction effect between grade and self-down activity was not significant.
10. Students coming from high SES and low SES groups were almost the same as far as creative thinking ability was concerned. The interaction effect between grade and SES was not significant.
11. Certain characteristics of creative children were: (i) courage in convictions, (ii) curiosity, (iii) independence in judgment, (iv) independence in thinking, (v) preoccupation with tasks, (vi) strongly intuitive, (vii) unwillingness to accept routine solutions of problems, (viii) willingness to take risks, and (ix) imaginative.

I. Studies Related to Conceptual Clarity of Critical Thinking

Wright, (1990) in his research on *"Critical thinking: Definition, measurement and development in vocational students in further education"*, (U.K.) stressed the need that teachers in further Education should strive to improve creative thinking abilities so that vocational studies are better prepared for making complex decisions in the work situation. In this respect the research has specific aims: first, to provide an operational definition of critical thinking, amendable to experimentation;

second, to develop a measure for creative thinking abilities; fourth, to determine the teaching style which might influence has been explained as judicious use of 'skepticism' tempered by 'reflection' and exp. It is productive of a more satisfactory solution to, or insight into a problem.

In the second aim, 'Reflective Skepticism' is shown to require high ability for differentiation AND integration of subject knowledge, differentiating ability being measured by a REP Test Grid, modified by writer to make it suitable for use with students from a wide variety of vocational subjects and integrating ability being measure by analyzing students' written response to questions about a number of items initially constructed teste passages which controls insufficient information to allow complete answers to the questions.

In the third aim, a hypothetico-deductive experiment was used to find out significant increases in students' critical thinking following exp with a package of thinking exercises. Results have shown that whereas students' differentiating abilities were high and remained unchanged by treatment, low integrating abilities were significantly improved in half the student groups following their exp with the thinking exercises.

In the fourth aim, action research methods were used to reduce how teaching styles might enhance critical thinking. Student's preferences for a range of teacher-directed and student-directed methods were obtained by a questionnaire before teaching demonstrations of transmission and interpretation styles were used to stimulate student discussions about different teaching methods. Results have shown that students preferred a flexible exposure to both teacher-directed and student-directed methods and this encouraged the development of integrating skills needed to enhance creative thinking.

Stahl, Nancy, (1990) has conducted a study on *"Developing criteria for a critical thinking program using the Delphi technique"* at Arizona State University.

The purpose of the study were: (1) to drive consensual definitions and characteristics of creative thinking, and (2) to use these definitions and characteristics as criteria for analyzing four existing thinking skills programs toward the selection of an appropriate creative thinking program for one particular school district.

After the review of the related literature, 18 definitions and 48 characteristics of creative thinking were considered as represent native examples of the wide variety of definitions and characteristics available to curriculum planners. From these two lists, then definitions and 25 characteristics were selected to be presented to the panel of experts who would rank these following the Delphi procedures. The criterion used in selecting the 10 definitions and 25 characteristics was to give the panel the wide variety of items from those available to make their decisions regarding the rank order. These experts consisted of 16 professional educators from one school district, including classroom teachers and administrators, who were familiar with creative thinking and the gifted program and who volunteered to participate in the study.

Eventually one definition and 16 characteristics of those provided on the third round questionnaires were selected via the consensus procedure inherent in the Delphi technique as the criteria that would be used to guidance the analysis of four thinking skills programs. This analysis would determine which, if any, program came closest including what these panelists considered should guide the development of a critical thinking program for their school district. The four programs which were considered were CORT, Philosophy for Children, Odyssey: A Curriculum for Thinking and Tactics for Thinking.

It was determined that all four programs were consistent with the one definition selected by the panel of experts. In the analysis of the programs using the 16 characteristics, it was found that Odyssey provided instruction consistent with 11 of these characteristics, more than any of the other programs although two other programs met nine each of the characteristics.

II. Creative Thinking and Related Variable

Burt, (1989) has conducted a research on the *"Identification of creative thinking variables in developmental testing and an experimental examination of the number and rules of participant in testing sessions"* at McGill University.

A large sample (N-206) of expert instructional designers were surveyed in order to determine how developmental testing is designed and conducted. The majority of respondents indicated that they did conduct formative testing of prototype instructional materials for purposes of revising them. Both one-to-one and small group testing were recommended with both the developer and the test subjects assuming active roles during the testing sessions. Both quantitative and qualitative (including attitudinal) data are gathered with an emphasis placed on the analysis of the post test data. Based on a review of the literature and the results of the survey, an experiment was conducted in order to investigate the effects of different roles that the participants might play during testing sessions with different numbers of participants might pay during testing sessions. Individuals assigned to small group did not produce as many comments during instruction as the one-to-one procedure. A content analysis of the qualitative data revealed that test subjects generally comment by indicating comprehension/recall problems. As a source of feedback, the attitudinal survey provided a considerable amount of data especially with small groups which were reluctant to make critical comments during instruction.

Riesenmy, (1991) has conducted a study on *"Retention and transfer of children's self-directed creative thinking"* at Washington University.

The researcher's main contention was reported to determine whether fourth and fifth grade children who were taught self-directed creative thinking skills could retain the skills and whether they could apply them to new problems that were different from the training problems. Children were taught the roles of Task Definer, Strategist, Monitor and Challenger and used them in a series of twelve small group discussions. This allowed each child to play the four thinking roles three times. The small groups discussed "everyday" problems that were designed to stimulate creative thinking and were held under the supervision of the children's classroom teacher.

Of the original for experiment and thirty control children who were to participate in this study, thirty-eight of the experimental and twenty-eight of the control subjects provided complete and usable data. All children were tested individually prior to the start of the small group discussions by one of four research staff members. One-third of each group (experimental and control) was assigned at random to one of three retention intervals; immediate, four week, or eight week. At the appropriate time, the child was tested again with a different but comparable problem to the one used as a pre-test.

Two transfer problems were selected to test children on an individual basis. One was a lateral transfer task and the other was a vertical transfer task. Both transfer problems were administered to the child in the same session as his or her retention problem.

Hypotheses predicted that the experimental children would outperform the control of children on the individual post test problems across all three retention intervals, and on both transfer tasks.

Results of the study showed that the experimental children earned superior retention scores on three variables compared to control children use of self-directed thinking skills, amount of information used in solution, and quality of answer. Experimental children also scored better than the control children on the two transfer problems.

Bates, (1991) has conducted a study on *"Effect of a systematic inquiry intervention on the critical thinking skills of a sample of master's degree student"* at the American University.

This study examined the effect of a systematic inquiry intervention, Systematic Inquiry: The Care and Feeding of a Research Idea (SI), on the creative thinking skills, as assessed through the WAtson-Glaser creative thinking Appraisal (CTA), of a sample of master's degree students. An experimental study was conducted using pre-test/post-test design.

The four hypotheses tested in this study stated that the mean post test CAT score of the experimental group was significantly higher than that of the control group. They also stated that there wold be significant improvement in the mean post-test score of the experimental group over the mean pre-test score of the experimental group and that there would be no significant improvement in the mean post-test score of the control group when they were controlled to that group's mean pre-test score.

The sample was nonrandom volunteer sample of 44 American University master's degree students which was divided into randomly selected experimental and control groups. Data were collected on gender, age, and educational background of sample members. All sample members were pre-test using the CAT, Form A. The experimental group ws exposed to SI. Both the experimental and control groups were post-tested using the CAT, Form B, Pre-test and post-test data were then compared within and between groups.

The results supported two for the null hypotheses. These hypotheses were that there would be significant difference the experiment group pre-test and post-test means and that there would be no significant difference between the experimental groups post-test mean and the control group post-test mean.

The results supported two of the research hypotheses. These were that the mean pre-test CAT score of the experimental group would not differ significantly from the mean pre-test CAT score of the control group and that the mean pre-test CAT score for the control group would not differ significantly from their mean post-test CAT (Critical Thinking Appraisal) score. The level for statistical significance was .05. The conclusion was drawn that showed no significant effect on the development of creative thinking skills in the master's degree students studied.

Rogers, (1991) has conducted a study on "*Creative thinking and intellectual development: A study of the effect of an integrated first year curriculum in science, engineering, and mathematics*", at Indiana State University. The purpose of this study was to assess the outcomes related to intellectual development and creative thinking of an innovative freshman year curriculum after its first year of implementation at Rose-Hulman Institute of Technology. The curriculum is a broad-based, integrated curriculum in which the material traditionally offered in a first-year engineering curriculum (physics, calculus, chemistry, computer science, graphics, engineering statics, and engineering design courses) are unified in a three course, twelve credits per quarter, sequence. The primary goals of the curriculum were to infuse concepts, improve techniques, and cultivate effective search strategies.

Students were pre-tested at the beginning of the academic year using the Watson-Galser Creative Thinking Appraisal (WGCTA) to assess creative thinking skills and the Cognitive Complexity Index of the Learning Environment Preferences (LEP) to assess intellectual development. A comparison group was selected using a cluster analysis technique which clustered students in the traditional curriculum with students participating in the experimental program based on demographic data and pre-test scores. At the end of the academic year, both groups were post-tested using the WGCTA and the LEP. The-tests were utilized to analyze the data.

It was found that after the first year there was no significant difference on measures of intellectual development and creative thinking between students in the experimental program and those in the comparison group who were in the traditional freshman curriculum. However, because of the complexity of the variables examined, the fact that the students in experimental program were highly selected, and the two groups tested were very homogeneous, it is recommended that further study be cone to examine the long-term effects of the program.

III. Comparative and Correletion Studies or Creative Thinking

Haboush, (1989) has conducted a study on "*An evaluation of Student learning outcomes under a creative thinking-social studies program*" at the University of New Jeresy.

The purpose of this investigation was to contribute to the field of professional psychology by expanding the existing knowledge based on critical thinking programs. Despite widespread claims that such programs may enhance academic performance and promote students' engagement within the instructional process, prior accounts of creative thinking programs have been largely descriptive in nature, lacking any empirical evaluation. For the present study, the development, implementation and evaluation of a Problem Solving Project and incorporating application of Elias and Clabby's (1989) 371 middle school students (grades six through eight) from a small, multiethnic, central New Jersy school district. During the 1986-1987 academic year, 172 students received their regular course of social studies instruction. Data were collected on: (a) the extent on seven report card variables was compared. Experimental students obtained significantly higher average levels of social studies achievement grades, language arts those marking periods that the program was in effect. Program implementation data revealed that considerable variability existed among experimental classes and suggested the importance of teachers' comfort with the sections are utilized in developing several alternative approaches to formalizing temporal persistence.

"Temporal persistence is initially formalized using circumscription to minimize "potential causes" of change, while every change is required to have a cause, facts are thereby permitted to persist whenever there is not "known" potential cause of their change. To illustrate its generality, we extend this approach to more expressive temporal formalisms, which support variable-duration persistence, ramifications, and causation. To escape unwarranted presumptions discovered in this first approach, as well as in all previous alternatives, another approach is developed that minimizes "unjustified" changes of persisting facts, where justified changes are defined in terms of the types of explicit knowledge that can justify them. It is shown that circumscriptive theories will require some such supplementation with autoepistemic notions to fully avoid unwarranted presumptions. Finally, this approach is also extended to a more expressive temporal theory including variable duration persistence and time-delays.

The results achieved contribute to our philosophical understanding of commonsense reasoning, provide a solution to the "frame problem" in artificial intelligence, and lay clear logical foundations for the construction of more expressive and robust automated commonsense reasoning systems.

Selman, (1989) has conducted a study on *"Critical thinking, rationality, and social practices"* at University of British Columbia.

Critical thinking is a widely shared educational goal which has been granted more explicit attention than ever in recent years. Five major approaches to this are of educational concern has been influential to the development of educational practices, research programs, and conceptualization in the field. Three of these approaches (the 'process' or basic skills approach, the problem solving approach, and the logic approach) are found to be based on unfounded assumptions about the nature of reasoning and thinking, and inadequate attention to the purposes which make critical thinking such a widely accepted educational goa. A fourth (the information processing approach) is found to involve instances of reduction which render incoherent of the terms with which we understand and assess our own reasoning, and that of others. The fifth approach (the multi-aspect approach associated with Robert Ennis) is not side effects essentially flawed, but is the reference of 'mental abilities' (which is essential for the issue of generalizability of creative thinking abilities) and with understanding the relationship between judgment and the other aspects of critical thinking.

It is argued that writers in the field of critical thinking generally have tried to purchase objectivity for their, conceptions by connecting them with the ideal of disengaged knowledge, either as exemplified by the study of formal logic or the natural sciences. It is argues that, in contrast with this approach, we ought to recognize that values and value judgments are at the heart of critical thinking.

The ideas of disengagement tends to interfere with our understanding of thinking as a normative (rule-governed) activity grounded in our social practices. This thesis argues for the adoption of a realist position with regard to values, an expressivity understanding of language, an interpretive stance toward the study of rationality, and a social constructive conception of rules. Some consequences of these positions for instruction, teacher preparations, and future research are suggested.

Eckberg, (1989) has conducted a study on *"Perception of control of environment and its relation to the acquisition of critical thinking and conflict resolution skills"* at University of Minnesota.

This study analyzed the "locus of control" perceptions of 544 tenth grade students enrolled in 32 world studies classes taught by seven teachers at two high schools in a suburban area. The design involved two phases. Phase one was a correlational survey of several background variables (student records of scholastic ability, socioeconomic status, past success in social studies, etc.) to see if they would be mediated by social attitudes ("external locus of control") as measured by the Rotten Internal-External Locus of Control Sale (E) and "personal incapacity" as measured by Mackey Personal Incapacity Scale (PI) in producing academic outcomes (dependent variables): critical thinking skills performance, conflict final exam, social studies course grade). Phase two involved an experiment to study whether control perceptions could be enhanced through a four session instructional treatment in conflict resolution strategies.

One of the results indicated that the E and PI scores are measuing some what different dimensions of response. In phase one, most of all variables correlated in the hypothesized direction with control perceptions; but, while statistically significant, the relationships were so low that there was no practical significance. Stepwise multiple regressions revealed a student's ability and past performance to be especially accurate predictors of score on the three dependent variables, but some statistically significant relationships emerged with E, PI, and socio-economic states.

In phase two, there was no more significant reduction in the E scores of the experimental group after the instructional treatment than in the control group. Multivariable analysis revealed significant interaction between E scores, ability scores, and father's occupation in the pretest to post test interval.

While weak correlations do not provide mandates for educational practice, one implication of concern to schools would be relationship between these measures of efficacy and socio-economic status. And while the present study suggests that scholastic ability and past grades are the best predictors of future social studies performance, the attitude mediating variables may have some effect, particularly on skills. More sensitive measures including anecdotal records, longer treatment time and special analyses of extreme E and PI scoring students would be likely area for investigation in future studies.

Jordon, (1990) has conducted a study on *"The relationship among reading comprehension, critical thinking, and metacomprehension and the effects of metacomprehensive strategic training"* at Memphis State University.

The purpose of this study was to investigate the relationship among critical thinking reading comprehension and metacomprehension and to examine the effectiveness of metacomprehension strategy training on the reading comprehension, critical thinking, and reading awareness abilities of students in grades four, five and six.

Major findings indicated positive correlations among

reading comprehension, critical thinking and metacomprehension with the strongest correlations being between reading comprehension and critical thinking. Students in the experimental group received significantly higher scores than did those in the control group in the areas of inferential comprehension and reading awareness. An analysis of scores by level of reading ability and by level of reading awareness indicated that students with higher levels performed significantly better in critical thinking, reading comprehension, and reading awareness.

Conclusions based on the analysis of data indicated the following: There is a positive relationship among metacomprehension, critical thinking, and reading comprehension. However, metacomprehensive training appears to have little effect on the literal and total reading comprehension and critical thinking scores of students in grades four, five, and six. On the other hand, metacomprehensive training appears to have a positive significant effect on the inferential reading comprehension and metacomprehensive abilities of students in grades four, five, and six. Additonally, students with hight levels of reading awareness are more likely to score higher on reading comprehension and critical thinking tasks. Also students with higher levels of reading ability perform significantly better than those with low ability on metacomprehension and critical thinking tasks.

Major implications of this study are that metacomprehensive skills cnabe effectively taught in the on context of the regular curriculum. Aditionally, both reading comprehension and critical thinking skills are affected by general metacomprehensive ability. Therefore, both reading comprehension and Critical thinking skills could be expected to increase as a result of extended metacomprehension strategy training.

McGarrity, (1990) has conducted a study on *"A study of the relationships of academic achievement, program preparation creative thinking ability , and classrom performance of preservice teachers in two selected universities in Georgia"* at Emory University.

There is considerable public concern for the quality of American education. Numerous articles, reports, and studies focus on the weaknesses of our educational system confidence has been shaken by the complimentary reports of teachers' incompetence and their students lack of achievement (Boyer, 1983; Weaver, 1970). Teacher educators are being forced to examine their selection procedure and preparation of future teachers.

It appears that there are schools of thought in regard to the selection, training, and evaluation of preservice teachers. One school of though suggests that brighter, more academically able preparation program (type, length and the inclusion of a critical thinking component in the preservice (Cargenie Commission, 1986; Holmes Group, 1986; Scho, 1989; Wise, 1986). The third school of though emphasizes that classroom performance identifies the effective teachers (Capie, 1985; Piper & Houston, 1980).

This study was designed to determine the best predictors of preservice teachers' perfomance on the Georgia Teacher Performance Assessment Instrument (TPAI) and to examine the relationships of (1) academic achievement, (2) program preparation, (3) critical thinking ability, (4) perceptions of critical thinking ability, (5) perceptions of the quality of one's preparation program and (6) classroom performance. The sample consisted of 49 preservice teachers from two universities in Georgia.

Stepwise regression analysis suggests that academic achievement, the type of preparation program, and perception of the quality of one's program were the significant predictors of TPAI scores. Pearson correlations are also found that preservice teachers' earning higher GPAs and rating higher the quality of their preparation were more successful on their performance-based assessments. The subjects' critical thinking scores or perceptions of critical thinking ability were not significantly related to the other variables and did not predict TPAI scores. Supplement analyses revealed that the predictors of TPAI scores changed when the sample was sorted by certification level or university. Hopefully, the results will aid those who recruit, train, and evaluate teachers. McGarrity, 1990.

Huesken, (1991) has conducted a study on *"the relationship between pricipals' self-perceived leadership in the teaching of critical thinking skills and students' analytical thinking"* at Temple University. There were two major objectives in this study concerning the following significant questions: (1) What were the common characteristics of those schools successful on the Analytical Thinking section of Pennsylvania's Educational Quality Assessment in comparison with those schools which were not as successful on the EQA? And (2) What were the common characteristics of the building principals' leadership and support in those schools successful on the Analytical Thinking section of the EQA versus those schools not as successful on the EQA?

Samples were established for study from a population of Pennsylvania high schools with scores in grade 11 on the EQA's Analytical Thinking section in 1987-88 that satisfied one and/or two criteria. First, schools were admitted to the sample if they demonstrated student scores above or below their prediction bands for Analytical Thinking. Second, schools were also included if they reflected student scores in the highest or lowest quartile in a percentile ranking.

The following list of conclusions were found to be characteristics of those schools and their principals with successful student results on the EQA's Analytical Thinking sections: (1) Faculty perception of the principal's leadership is significantly greater. (2) Class size is significantly smaller. (3) Students perform significantly better on other standardized tests of cognitive skills, such as Reading Comprehension, Writing Skills, and Mathematics, and noncognitive measures of students self-concept. (4) There are significantly fewer principals with 15 years or more in their current building positions. (5) The principals report significantly more effective behaviours in the task areas of communications, curriculum, staff development, and supervision. (6) The level of role responsibilty is a more significant measurement of effective principal behaviour than the frequency of role performance. (7) The task area of communications is a more significant concern for principals.

John Follman, (1992) through his study representative critical thinking correlations reprised over even of these indicates that the construct of critical thinking is the lesser known and lesser investigated construct of critical reading. It is much stronger with reading enough to moderate with the school aptitude (IQ) Language, verbal vocabulary, intelligence ability, the progressive presence of language, verbal ability in critical thinking cannot be denied and efforts to enhance critical thinking should exploit the enhancement of their language ability.

IV. Studies related to the Developmental of Critical Thinking Skills

Kehler Merita Trice, (1982) has conducted a study on *"The effects of programme for gifted High School students on critical thinking and the association of thisvariable to intelligence, sex, academic achievement and teachers rating of behavioural characteristics"* at East Texas State University.

This study sought to determine of high school students who participated in a special program for the fighted made significant, improvement in critical thinking. The difference were compared by sex, specific school attendance, academic achievement, intelligence and critical thinking. The sample consisted of 132 high school students who participated in the first 5 years of the programme. The data from the pre-test and post-test of the Watson-Glacer critical thinking appraisal, the science research associates, achievement series and the scales for rating the behavioural characteristics of superior students, were analyzed by the t- test for correlated scores, the t-test for independent means, the ANCOVA the F test and the Chi square test., were used to test the hypotheses.

The major findings of the studies were:

1. There was significant gain in critical thinking irrespective of sex.
2. There was significant difference found between high and low critical thinkers on all areas of academic achievement and abilities.
3. The reading was the only academic area which indicates a significant difference between students rated s low in gifted characteristics or high in gifted characteristics.

Werback, Judith Rea, (1984) has conducted a study on *"A*

Theoritical model for a staff development programme for teaching elementary students. The process of evaluation as a critical thinking skills" at Georgia Univerisity.

This study was concerned with the creation of a model for a staff development programme which could prepare educators to teach elementary school students the process of evaluation as a segment of critical thinking skills. The study included analysis and synthesis of theoretical considerations as well as suggested strategies for practical application.

The process for developing the model involved the following phases.

1. A survey and analysis of literature in the areas of evaluation, critical thinking skills, selected learning theories, and staff development.
2. Identification of major assumptions in the areas of critical thinking, evaluation and staff development.
3. A synthesis of the data into a model for staff development.
4. Statement of conclusions, derived from the model.

The model integrated emphasis on collaborative planning, active involvement, competent leadership, theories concerning adult education, and provision of adequate resources and rapport through out the seven stages included, Initiation, Planning, Orientation, Education, Evaluation, Implementation and Assessment.

The educational stage of the model was specified for three years in order to allow for the internalization of the complex and sophisticated learnings concerning the process of evaluation. The educational stage specified component skills of evaluation including feedback, questioning skills, criteria use and development data collection and analysis goal setting and evaluation, judgment, decision making and problem solving.

The following conclusions concerning the process of evaluation were drawn from the study.

1. The process of evaluation is an integral component of critical thinking.
2. Thinking skills are basic to learning.

3. Specific strategics involved in critical thinking and the process of evaluation, such as question asking and the use of appropriate criteria can be learned.
4. Thinking skills including the process of evaluation can be integrated into staff development programs and its educational process during the elementary school years at simple, but very basic level. Recommendations were made concerning related areas which warrant further investigation.

Byrne, Jones, (1984) has conducted a study on *"The effect of critical thinking skills instruction on achievement and attitude of elementary students differing in learning style preferences"* at Vergenia University.

The purpose of this study was to determine the effect of teacher paced vs. self paced instruction of critical thinking skills on the achievement of higher level thinking process and student attitudes in elementary students with a high, moderate, or low preference for teacher-structured learning.

Fifth grade students (n=35) were randomly assigned to three groups in two elementary schools, two treatment and one control using a random block design based on abilities or intelligence and verbal analogy achievement.

1. The direct teaching of the skills rather than the methodology was the significant factor in greater achievement. Scores on measures of critical thinking not directly related to the instruction and program did not show significant differences between groups, suggesting no transfer occurred in the ability to perform thinking tasks not specifically instructed.
2. Althogh there were indications that a preference for self paced self structure learning resulted in

higher achievement, the results were not statistically significant. A match between learning style preferences and teaching methodology did not result in greater achievement.

3. Attitudes of students toward institutions of thinking skills were not affected significantly by teaching methodology nor by differing learning style preferences.

Hudgins and Edelman, (1986) has conducted a study on

"Teaching critical thinking skills to fourth and fifth graders through teacher led small group discussions" at Washington University.

This study was designed to increase fourth and fifth grade pupils critical thinking skills. Teachers led nine critical thinking discussions with a group composed of six members of their class. The pre-lesson was taught immediately prior to two interstice workshops for the teachers and it provided borderline data against which to evaluate changes in teacher – pupil behaviour following the workshops. Analysis of the audiotape recordings revealed that, compared to the precise, teachers talk is significantly less during the discussions and pupils spoke significantly more. After the precision pupils offered evidence for the opinion of conclusion significantly more offers than simply advanced conclusions, substituted or not. Although the amount of teacher talk declared dramatically, there is no accompanying shift in the categories of talk they used to stimulate children's critical thinking. The major findings of the study are:-

1. The teachers can significantly reduce their vertical dominations of the groups, but still they can maintain the group functions.
2. By encouraging the children to discuss more in

the group that helps them to do more critical thinking.

Griffit, Donald, (1987) has conducted a study on *"The effect of activity-oriented science instruction on the development of critical thinking skills and achievement"* at Northern Arizona University.

The purpose of this study was to determine whether students instructed in the activity oriented method developed a higher lever of thinking skills and achievement than students instructed in the traditional text book recitation approach.

An experimental group of third and sixth grade students was instructed using an activity-oriented approach while a control group of similar students was instructed by means of traditional text boo recitation method. Both groups were taught using the same science units over a twelve-week period of time.

Both groups received the Cornell critical thinking test. Level X (CCTT) and the science subset of the Stanford Achievement Test (SAT) as a pre test and post test. The results were analyzed using separate t-tests analysis of Variance. The findings of the study reveals that there was no significant difference in teaching method in terms of developing critical thinking skills. However, there was a significant difference with respect to science achievement at both grades levels. Students instructed in the activity oriented approach showed significant growth over those instructed using the text book method. The variable gender and grade level indicated that gender was of no significance to the study and neither grade level significantly out performed the other.

Hudgins and Edelman, (1988) has conducted a study on

"Children's Self-Directed critical thinking" at Washington University.

The major purpose of the study is the develop directed critical thinking through the teaching of four roles namely (a) task definition (b) strategy formulation (c) monitoring progress and (d) challenging or verifying observations of others. The fourth role was developed specifically because of the small group discussion format, which was employed in the experimental phase of the study.

These elementary schools located in the same public school district were the source of the sample for the research. Experimental children were drawn from the classes of the 5 teachers two fourth and three fifth grade who had agreed to participate in the study control children were related from one fourth and one fifth grade class in the third elementary school in the same school district. All the pupils in those seven classes (four experimental and two control classes) were given a test of critical thinking that was to be used for purposes of matching experimental and control children. There were 20 students in each control & experimental group.

Matching between the experimental group and the control group was thus a matter of enquiry that the best means and standard elevations of the two did not differ significantly.

All children were given a problem to solve in an individual interview setting children in the experimental group participated subsequently in eight small group discussions in which they learned and applied "self directed critical thinking" skill. After the small group discussions all the children were again listed individually on a problem comparable to the first.

The major finding of the study is that the children in the experimental group were significantly higher than those in the control group when scores for (a) applications of the thinking skills (b) amount of relevant information used to solve the problem and (c) quality of answer.

Johnson, (1989) has conducted a study on "*Learning to be a resonsive teacher: Assisting student performance during class discussion to enhance critical thinking*" at University of California.

The study was a microgenetic process analysis of one teacher, the author, who sought to learn how best to assist the performance of herstudnets during class discussion. The class discussions were videotaped, the tapes were transcribed, and the transcriptions along with the videotapes were analyzed for patterns in behavioural change which were beneficial and those which were deleterious to discussion. A journal and fieldnotes were also used as sources of data for analysis. At the conclusion of the study, the analysis documented specific behavioral changes which need to occur to promote the critical thinking of one's students while engaged in classroom dialogue.

Provaznik Eble, (1991) has conducted a study on "*Analysis of teachers' and children's verbal self-directed critical thinking small-group discussion*" at Washington University, presents an analysis of verbal teacher and student behaviour as it occurred in a quasi-experimental study of children thinking. The purpose of the study is to provide a research base for the in-service teachers participating in future studies of children's critical thinking. Ten fourth and fifth grade teachers each met with a group consisting of four of their students to solve every day different kinds of problems. The teacher training discouraged teachers from dominating the discussion. Teachers were instructed to facilitate discussion encouraging children to use the information in the study to solve the problems.

Each group participated in twelve discussions. Those of the total 120 tapes were selected; three for each teacher. The tapes with grouped in three samples. The first sample includes problems in the first third of the intervention; the second sample contains the second third, and the third sample problems from the last third.

The analysis reveal several outcomes: (1) The amount of teacher's talk diminishes over the twelve lesson, and the amount of pupils talk increases in a reciprocal manner. (2) The number of discussions initiated by students increases significantly. (3) All four of thinking roles are played within each of the ten small groups is learnt of the discussions sampled. (4) The increase in the option of student utterances that are classified as role playing is significant. (5) The percentage of story element used does change across the three samples of role playing and the student utterances of the use of evidence. (6) The proportion of teacher structuring does not change significantly.

The implications for future in-service of teachers with children's self-directed critical thinking discussions groups are discussed and to gain a more thorough understanding of the manner in which those methods came to be chosen as part of the teacher's repertoire. The value in studying teaching behavior becomes clear when they are viewed as end-products or artifacts of the learning to teach process.

This study differs from others in that the interviews delayed beyond the identification of where teachers obtained their ideas for methods employed in the class room. The importance of the participants' philosophies of teaching emerged as a significant factor affecting teaching style.

Current issues in teacher education reform are addressed. Many of the final recommendations were generated directly by the participating teachers. Other recommendations were developed by synthesizing common concerns.

The results shows that learning to teach is more complex than socialization or finding sources for ideas. The individual teacher must be considered an integral part of the process.

Chennault, (1989) has conducted a study on "*Enhancing critical thinking skills in gifted elementary school students*" at Mississippi State University.

This study was designed to determine if significant differences existence in the adjusted mean scores in critical thinking for a group of fifth grade and sixth-grade gifted students who participated in critical thinking strategies curriculum and a group fifth – and sixth grade students who participated in a traditional gifted classroom curriculum. The length of time (3 years or less versus greater than 3 years) students and participated in the gifted program was also considered.

The subjects were 72 fifth- and sixth-grade students from a school district of 33,000 students in central Mississippi. The research design was pre-test-post-test non randomized control group design utilizing a 2x2 factorial analysis of covariance. The Ennis-Weir Critical Thinking Essay Test was administered to the control and treatment groups as a pre-test and post-test. The treatment consisted of a 7-week curriculum of critical thinking skills designed by the researcher which contained objectives related to differentiating fact and opinion; defining and utilizing propaganda, bandwagon, and repetition techniques; sequencing information, using deductive reasoning to support opinions; etc. This control grou was taught a curriculum traditionally in the gifted classes during the 7-week period.

Statistically significant differences were found in the adjusted mean scores in critical thinking for the students who had the traditional gifted curriculum and those students who had the critical thinking strategies curriculum. The adjusted mean scores revealed that the students with the critical thinking scores for the two groups regarding length of participation time in the gifted program or for the interaction of type of curriculum and length of time in the gifted program or for the interaction of type of curriculum and length of time in the gifted program.

Ferrell, (1991) in her study on *"critical thinking as a function of teacher questions"* at Georgia University, focused much on the teachers involvement in developing critical thinking. Present–day educators attach more importance to the teaching critical thinking skills. While general consensus maintains the importance of these skills, differing views exist regarding the various methods of teaching which may contribute to the development of critical thinking skills in high school students. Five questions were asked in this study. The first question posed asked if teacher questioning could be altered to include more critical thinking questions. A second opinion involved the possible correlation between number of critical thinking questions asked and the resulting number of critical thinking answers given. Additional questions posed involved the effect of teacher responses on students and the impact of student participation in relation to the number of critical thinking questions asked by teachers. The final question posed was concerned with the performance of students on a standardized critical thinking test (Watson-Glaser Critical Thinking Appraisal) after they had been exposed to an alteration of teacher questions. Four average-level high school social studies classes were divided into two control classes and two treatment classes. Baselines were recorded for all classes. Teachers were trained in after school sessions on how to ask questions that elicit critical thinking responses. Class interactions were audiotaped in their entirety and coded for type of questions asked and type of responses given. Participation was recorded for each student. The results indicated that teacher questions were altered and more critical thinking questions were asked by teachers in treatment classes. There was a positive correlation between the number of critical thinking questions asked and the number of critical thinking responded given. No significant correlation was found between the level of participation of the students studied and the number of critical thinking responses given and the number of positive teacher responses given. There was a significant increase in the Watson-Glaser scores for students in the treatment classes but no such increase was noted for students in control classes.

Moreyra, (1991) has taken up a study on *"The role of thinking frames in developing teachers' critical thinking skills and disposition"* at Miami University.

The purpose of the study was to determine the role of thinking frames in developing teachers' critical thinking skills and dispositions. The subjects were elementary teachers who participated in a ten-week in-service programme. Treatments were randomly assigned to three groups. The experimental group received instruction in Richard Paul's Critical Thinking Remodeling of Lesson Plans with the inclusion of a thinking frame, a graphic representation of critical reflection. The comparison group received the same instruction with the exclusion of the thinking frame. The base-line group was instructed using a traditional approach which excluded both critical thinking skills and a thinking frame. The major findings of the study were as follows: (1) Teachers who were taught in the experimental group did not obtain statistically different scores on the Ennis-Weir Critical Thinking Essay Test than the teachers taught in the comparison or base-line groups; (2) Teachers across groups showed nonsignificant differences in how they perceived themselves as thinkers when measured by Edward's Self-Concept as a Thinner Scale; (3) Teachers in the experimental group reached a higher level of reflectivity as assessed by Van Manen's Levels of Reflectivity than teachers in the comparison and base-line groups. The results of one-way analysis of variance (ANOVA) at the .05 significance level revealed that there were no statistically significant differences. However,in the qualitative analysis of the data the results indicate that teachers in the experimental group reached a higher level of critical reflection. Thinking frames seem to be a process for helping teachers become more critically reflective. They facilitate understanding of the mental contructs and processes that underlie teacher behaviour, a must for the portrayal of cognitive theory in teachers' development. The discussion section offers valuable insights for educators interested in studying the complexity of teachers' thought processes and development of critical reflection. Recommendation for further research as well as the limitations of the study are included.

Kezer, (1991) has conducted a study on *"effects of computer technology and traditional methods of instruction upon the critical thinking skills of teachers and students"* at North Carlina University.

The purpose of this study was to investigate the effectiveness of computer technology in developing critical thinking skills of teachers and middle school students. The influence of years of teaching exp and educational, degrees held by the teacher upon teacher gains student gains were also investigated. In addition, this study examined the relationship between achievement test scores and critical thinking scores and critical thinking scores.

The sample consisted of 20 classroom teachers and 449 fifth and sixth grade students at a middle school in rural Piedmont North Carolina. Ten teachers and 239 students were in classrooms with computers, while the control group of 10 teachers and 210 students did not have computers.

At least for gain scores (post-test scores minus pre-test

scores) of the computer group with the control group indicated a significantly greater gain (p 0.0001) for computer students than non-computer students. Teacher gains were not significant.

A Pearson correlation revealed a significant (p .005) inverse relationship between years of teaching exp and student gain scores. Students of teachers with the fewest years of exp had thinking highest gain scores.

California Achievement Test (CAT) scores were compared with scores on the Cornell Critical Thinking (CCTT). The results of a regression analysis indicated that for all students in the sample (n=100), the CAT reading score was the best predictor of overall CCTT gain scores (p .03). CAT scores were less predictive at the sixth grade level than at the fifth.

Mean overall gain scores for the 20 individual classrooms ranged from1.04 the 6.4 with a mean of 2.4. An overview of classrooms based on teachers' logs and interview questions indicated that teachers in the classrooms with the highest gain scores treated critical thinking as a separate subject, used a cooperative learning approach, and used the computer for reinforcement but did not depend upon it to teach.

Rile, (1991) has done a study on *"Teachers questioning for improvement of critical thinking skills"* at Wisconsiss University.

The purpose of this study was to examine the impact of quality questions by a home economics teacher on the critical thinking abilities and achievement test scores of twelth grade high school students. This study is based on a conceptual framework which was developed to show relationship between the work of Dewey, Tennis, Burner and Bloom. A detailed three and one-half week curricular unit on aging was developed for use in this study. The experimental design included an experimental group (41) taught with the use of questioning techniques and a control group (30) taught in a traditional manner. Four null hypotheses were tested regarding difference in change of critical thinking scores or achievement test scores of home economics students taught with or without the use of higher level questioning techniques. Independent variables included whether students were identified as regular or special education. The Cornell Critical Thinking Test measures of critical thinking and achievement.

Repeated measures analysis of variance was utilized, using grade point average as a covariate, to test the hypotheses. Qualitative date was obtained from students and teachers.

Findings confirmed that the questioning technique did assist students to improve critical thinking ability (as measured by the Cornell Critical Thinking Test) for the experimental group. No significant differences were found between the special and regular education students within the experimental and control groups. The questioning technique did not make a significant impact on students' achievement test scores.

Recommendations were made regarding investigation of abilities of students with special learning needs to think critically, replication of the study, effects of student attitudes toward aging related to teachers asking questions, further development of the curricular unit, Enhancing Inter-generational Contact, and the process of infusing critical thinking into home economics content.

Implications of the related literature on the present study:

1. The correlational studies conducted in the area of critical thinking helped the researcher to identify the relevant variables and also to restrict to the essential and limited number of variables. The related literature also guided the researcher regarding classifying the variables like sex,

intelligence and SES into independent, dependent and moderator variables [Mc garrity 1990, Huesken 1991,John Föllman 1992, Burt 1989, Bates 1991…].

2. The studies conducted by McGarrity and others helped the researcher to consider the academic achievement as the dependent variable.
3. The researcher was able to acquaint with the names of different tools available regarding critical thinking skills such as Watson-Glaser critical thinking Appraisal [WGCTA] tool, Richard Paul's critical thinking Model, Cornell Critical Thinking Tests [CCTT]etc.
4. The major implications of the related study on the present research is the selection of the research design and the approaches to be followed while developing the programme of critical thinking [Snooke 1973, Moreyra 1991,Hudgins and Edelman1986], further the related literature has also helped for identifying the variables in terms of high and low groups. This knowledge has really helped the researcher to plan for factorial design which helps for finding the interaction effect.

Thus the present chapter dealt with the review of the related literature. The next chapter deals about the methodology followed by the researcher.

3

METHODOLOGY

In the previous chapter the researcher has reviewed some of the researches related to the present study. In the present chapter the methodology, i.e., the discussion of The variables, hypothesees, sampling procedure, tools and techniques of the research are discussed.

Statement of the Problem

"An impact of a progamme of critical thinking skills on the achievement of secondary school teacher trainees of Bangalore city."

The study as has been made clear in the statement has two phases. The first phase being developing the structured programme based on certain components of critical thinking skills. Like any other cognitive skill, critical thinking skills, may also have impact on the achievement of teacher trainee. Hence, the Phase II is to find out the effect of certain moderator variables like sex, intelligence and socio-economic status, not only on the academic achievement of the teacher trainees but also on the development of the critical thinking skills. Hence in this study such of those variables as are related to critical thinking skills and also to academic achievement are considered by the researcher.

Operational Definitions

In this study critical thinking skills concern with the abilities to deal reasonably and reflectively with questions regarding clarification, inferring, investigation, making value judgment by establishing the relationship between previous exp and the new situation.

The six components of the critical thinking skills that are suggested by Terry Applegate and Anitha Harnadek are considered. They are:

1. Distinguishing relevant from irrelevant information, cliam or reasons.
2. Determining the factual accuracy of a statement.
3. Determining the credibility of a source.
4. Identifying unstated assumptions.
5. Determining the strength of an argument or a claim.
6. Distinguishing between verifiable facts and value claim.

Socio-Economic Status

It refers to the actual status of a person in the Society which is measured in terms of family income, education and occupation. The person will be placed in different categories based on the above three items

Intelligence

It refers to the general mental ability.

Teacher Trainees

It refers to the students who are studying in different Colleges Education offering BEd course in Bangalore city.

Programme

This refers to the programme developed by the investigator based on the selected six components of critical thinking skills.

Achievement

Achievement refers to performance of teacher trainees in the test of methods of teaching Physics.

Discussion of Variables

A variable is a symbol to which numerals or values are assigned (Kerlinger, 1969). A variable is a characteristic, which in given project can have more than one value (Fox, 1969). According to Tuckman (1978), a variable is that factor which is measured,manupulated and observed by the investigator. There are different types of variables namely independent, dependent, moderator variable etc.

An independent variable is one in which prediction can be done. the variables that are studied are called dependent variables. Where as moderator variables are those which influence both independent and dependent variables.

Based on the studies conducted in the area of critical thinking skills, the following variables were selected for this study keeping the objectives of the study.

(a) Critical thinking skills(Critical thinking skills)

(b) Sex

(c) Socio-economic Status

(d) Intelligence

(e) Achievement

Keeping the problem and the objectives of the study, the above five variables were classified under dependent, independent and moderator variables.

Independent Variable

In this study critical thinking skill is considered as an independent variable, because this skill is operational to influence the achievement of the teacher trainees.

Dependent Variable

Achievement in methods of teaching physics is considered as a dependent variable in the present study, because the achievement of the trainees may be influenced by the critical thinking skills.

Moderator Variables

Sex, SES and intelligence are considered as moderator variables because

> They influence both the critical thinking skills (independent variable) andAcademic achievement (independent variable) and academic achievement (dependent variable).

Hypotheses

The following major and minor null hypotheses have been formulated keeping in mind the objectives and the variables under consideration.

Major Hypotheses

1. There is no significant difference between the pretest and post test mean scores of experimental and control group regarding critical thinking skills based on achievement in methods of teaching physics.
2. There is no significant difference between pre test and post test mean scores of the control regarding critical thinking skills based on achievement in methods of teaching physics.
3. There is no significant difference between the pre test mean scores of the experimental group and post test mean scores of the control group regarding Critical thinking skills based on achievement in methods of teaching physics.
4. There is no significant difference between the post

test mean scores of the experimental group and the control group regarding Critical thinking skills based on achievement in methods of teaching physics.

5. There is no significant interaction between the nature of test Sex. SES & intelligence regarding Critical thinking skills based on achievement in methods of teaching physics.
6. There is no significant interaction between Sex, SES, intelligence and critical thinking skills based on the achievement in methods of teaching physics.
7. There is no significant difference between pre test and post test scores of the programme of Critical thinking skills based on achievement in methods of teaching physics.
8. There is no significant difference in the achievement in methods of teaching physics with reference to Sex, SES, intelligence and Critical thinking skills.
9. There is no significant difference between the total scores of Critical thinking skills with respect to Sex, SES and intelligence.

Minor Hypotheses

1.1: There is no significant difference between the pre test and post test mean scores of achievement in methods of teaching physics of experimental and control group regarding the component of Critical thinking skills namely *determining the relevance of information.*

1.2: There is no significant difference between the pre test and post test mean scores of achievement in methods of teaching physics of experimental and control group regarding the component of Critical thinking skills namely determining the accuracy of factual claim.

1.3: There is no significant difference between the pre test and post test mean scores of achievement in methods of teaching physics of experimental and control group regarding the component of critical thinking skill namely determining credibility of a source.

1.4: There is no significant difference between the pre test and post mean scores of achievement in methods of teaching physics of experimental and control group regarding the component of Critical thinking skills namely identifying the unstated assumption.

1.5: There is no significant difference between the pre test and post test mean scores of achievement in methods of teaching physics of experimental and control group regarding the component of Critical thinking skills namely determining the strength of an argument.

1.6: There is no significant difference between the pre test and post test mean scores of achievement in methods of teaching physics of experimental and control group regarding the component of Critical thinking skills namely distinguishing statement of fact from value judgment.

1.7: There is no significant difference between the pre test and post test mean scores of achievement in methods of teaching physics of experimental and control group regarding all the components of critical thinking skills.

2.1: There is no significant difference between pre test and post test mean scores of achievement in methods of teaching physics of control group regarding the component of Critical thinking skills namely determining the relevance of information.

2.2: There is no significant difference between pres test and post test mean scores of achievement in methods of teaching physics of control group regarding the component of Critical thinking skills namely determining the accuracy of actual claim.

2.3: There is no significant difference between pre test .and post test mean scores of achievement in methods of teaching physics of control group regarding the component of critical thinking skills namely determining the credibility of a source.

2.4: There is no significant difference between pretest and post test mean scores of achievement in methods of teaching physics of control group regarding the component of Critical thinking skills namely identifying the unstated assumption.

2.5: There is no significant difference between pre test post test mean scores of achievement in methods of teaching physics of control group regarding the component of Critical thinking skills namely determining the strength of an argument.

2.6: There is no significant difference between pre rest and post test mean scores of achievement in methods of teaching physics of control group regarding the component of critical thinking skills namely distinguishing statement of fact from value judgment.

2.7: There is no significant difference between pre test and post test mean scores of achievement in methods of teaching physics of control group regarding all the components of critical thinking skills.

3.1: There is no significant difference between the pre test mean scores of achievement in methods of teaching physics of the experimental group and post test mean scores of the control group regarding the component of critical thinking skills namely determining the relevance of information.

3.2: There is no significant difference between the post test mean scores of achievement in methods of teaching physics of the experimental group and the control group regarding the component of Critical thinking skills namely determining the accuracy of factual claim.

3.3: There is no significant difference between the post test mean scores of achievement in methods of teaching physics of the experimental group and the control group regarding the component of critical thinking skills namely determining the credibility of a sôurce

3.4: There is no significant difference between the post test mean scores of achievement in methods of teaching physics of the experimental group and the control group regarding the component of critical thinking skills namely identifying the unstated assumptions.

3.5: There is no significant difference between the post test mean scores of achievement in methods of teaching physics of the experimental group and the control group regarding the component of Critical thinking skills namely determining the strength of an argument.

3.6: There is no significant difference between the post test mean scores of achievement in methods of teaching physics of the experimental group and the control group regarding the component of

Critical thinking skills . namely distinguishing statement of fact from value judgment.

3.7: There is no significant difference between the post test mean scores of achievement in methods of teaching physics of the experimental group and the control group regarding all the components of Critical thinking skills

4.1: There is no significant difference between the post test mean scores of achievement in methods of teaching physics of the experimental group and the control group regarding the component of Critical thinking skills namely determining the relevance of information.

4.2: There is no significant difference between the post test mean scores of achievement in methods of teaching physics of the experimental group and the control group regarding the component Critical thinking skills namely determining the accuracy of factual claim.

4.3: There is no significant difference between the post test mean scores of achievement in methods of teaching physics of the experimental group and the control group regarding the component of Critical thinking skills namely determining the credibility of a source.

4.4: There is no significant difference between the post test mean scores of achievement in methods of teaching physics of the experimental group and the control group regarding the component of Critical thinking skills namely identifying the unstated assumption.

4.5: There is no significant difference between the post test mean scores of achievement in methods of teaching physics of the experimental group and the control group regarding the component of Critical thinking skills namely determining the strength of an argument.

4.6: There is no significant difference between the post test mean scores of achievement in methods of teaching physics of the experimental group and the control group regarding the component of Critical thinking skills namely distinguishing statement of fact from value judgment.

4.7: There is no significant difference between the post test mean scores of achievement in methods of teaching physics of the experimental group and the control group regarding all the components of critical thinking skills.

5.1: There is no significant interaction between the nature of test, Sex, SES & intelligence regarding the component of critical thinking skills namely determining the relevance of information.

5.2: There is no significant interaction between the nature of test, Sex, SES & intelligence regarding the component of critical thinking skills namely determining the accuracy of factual claim.

5.3: There is no significant interaction between the nature of test, Sex, SES and intelligence regarding the component of critical thinking skills namely determining the credibility of a source.

5.4: There is no significant interaction between the nature of test, Sex, SES and intelligence regarding the component of critical thinking skills namely identifying the unstated assumption.

5:5: There is no significant interaction between the nature of test, Sex, SES and intelligence regarding the component of critical thinking skills namely determining the strength of an argument.

5.6: There is no significant interaction between the nature of test, Sex, SES and intelligence regarding the component of critical thinking skills namely distinguishing statement of fact from value judgment.

5.7: There is no significant interaction between the nature of test, Sex, SES and intelligence regarding the achievement in methods of teaching physics.

6.0: There is no significant interaction between sex, SES, intelligence and critical thinking skills regarding the achievement in methods of teaching physics.

7.1: There is no significant difference between pretest and post test scores of the programme of critical thinking skills regarding the component namely determining the relevance of information.

7.2: There is no significant difference between the pre test and post test scores of the programme of critical thinking namely determining the accuracy of factual claim.

7.3: There is no significant difference between pre test and post test scores of programme of critical thinking skills regarding the component namely determining the credibility of a source.

7.4: There is no significant difference between pre test and post test scores of programme of critical thinking skills regarding the component namely identifying the unstated assumption.

7.5: There is no significant difference between pre test and post test scores of programme of critical thinking skills regarding the component namely determining the strength of an argument.

7.6: There is no significant difference between pre test and post test scores of programme of critical thinking skills regarding the component namely distinguishing statement of fact from value judgment.

7.7: There is no significant difference between pre test and post test scores of programme of critical thinking skills regarding all the components.

8.1: There is no significant difference in the achievement in methods of teaching physics of male and female teacher trainees.

8.2: There is no significant difference in the achievement in methods of teaching physics of high and low SES teacher trainees.

8.3: There is no significant difference in the achievement in methods of teaching physics of high and low intelligent teacher trainees.

8.4: There is no significant difference in the achievement in methods of teaching physics of high and low critical thinking skills of teacher trainees.

9.1: There is no significant difference between male and female teacher trainees regarding their scores on critical thinking skills.

9.2: There is no significant difference between high and low SES teacher trainees regarding their scores on critical thinking skills.

9.3: There is no significant difference between high and low intelligent teacher trainees regarding their scores on critical thinking skills.

Sampling

In any research, collecting the data from the whole population to arrive at generalization is impracticable. In addition, the use of the larger population will not help to measure all characteristics. By the time the researcher completes the measurement of certain characteristics it is quite possible that the population would have changed. Hence, there is a need on the part of the researcher to select a small portion of the population objectively. This small portion of population selected for observation, collection of data and analysis is called a sample.

A sample is a segment replica of a universe which is selected in a particular way by the researcher. A sample should represent the characteristics of population fairly and accurately. There are different types of sampling procedures used in researches.

1. Random Sampling (Probability Sampling)

It refers to any procedure in which each population element has a specificable likelihood or probability of being included in the sample. In most of the researches this type of sampling procedure is considered since it is based on objectivity.

2. Stratified Sampling

This type of sampling is used when the populatoin consists of number of subgroups or strata that may differ in the characteristics being studied. The strata may be age, sex, occupation, income etc.

3. Cluster Sampling or Area Sampling

When the population of interest is infinite and when the geographic distribution of the individuals is widely scattered, this technique is used.

It involves the selection of a sample of one kind of element actually selecting some larger unit which contains several units.

4. Controlled Sampling

It is one in which the selection is not left to chance, but in which the distribution of some selected characteristics is made to confirm to some predetermined proportion. It may or may not involve random selection.

5. Purposive Sampling

It is another form of non-probability sampling which is characterised by the use of judgment and a deliberate effort to obtain representative samples by including presumably typical areas or groups in the sample.

In the present study the researcher in interested in finding the impact of critical thinking skills on the achievement of (methods of teaching physics) secondary school teacher trainees. Therefore, he has selected the colleges of education which are located in Bangalore city where the trainees who have taken methods of teaching physics are studying. Hence the present study involves purposive sampling technique. The size of the sample is 125 which includes all the trainees who have taken methods of teaching physics as their methods. 960 in experimental group and 60 in control group (initially)]. The sample is selected from four aided colleges of education.

Tools Used for the Study

Research tools are very essential in any research to collect the data. The selection of standardized test helps in minimizing the possibility of collecting the irrelevant data. The selection of the tool should be given primary importance in any research. Hence, keeping the objectives of the study and the variables selected, the researcher has used the following tools to collect the data related to the study.

Socio-economic Status Scale

It refers to the actual status of the person in the society which is measured in terms of his income, education and occupation. In order to find the socio-economic status of a person, his income, educational level and occupations are considered.

(a) Educational status: It refers to the actual status of the person in the society by the virtue of his educational qualification.

(b) Occupational status: It is a position one occupies in the society by virtue of his education.

(c) Economic status: It refers to the position occupied by the individual in the society by virtue of his income.

For these categories, suitable weightages are given. The total weightage given to all these categories given an index which indicates the socio-economic status.

There are many scales available to measure SES like those developed by Pareek and Trivedi, Kulshrestha, Kruppuswamy etc. The investigators has selected the socio-economic status scale developed by Kuppuswamy because, it has been standardized using the urban population. This scale being a simple one involves easy scoring procedure. In addition to this, the scale has higher reliability and validity. Keeping the recent pay revision scales in mind the investigator has modified it further by trying it out to a group of students and established validity and reliability (0.85). This tool was used to collect data regarding SES of teacher trainees.

Raven's Progressive Matrices (RPM)

It is a non-verbal culture free test of intelligence. It can be used for both high school and college students. The test consists of five sub-tests namely A,B,C,D and E. Under each sub test there are twelve figures. Against each incomplete pattern, six possible figures are given. Among these one will be the most suitable figure to complete the large figure. The complexity of a test increases from test A to E. This test has high reliability (0.71) and validity. The scores obtained by the trainees can be grouped and interpreted in terms of high intelligence, average intelligence and below average intelligence using the conversion table of the progressive matrices.

Achievement

The achievement test has been prepared taking the four broad units of B.Ed. methods of teaching physics syllabus. The four units chosen among the 8 units of the syllabi require greater amount of the use of higher cognitive ability as well as they include the ideas of the remaining four units. The four units are planning lessons in physics, methods of teaching physics, media and activities and evaluation in physics. The investigator constructed pre-test and post-test both in the above quoted areas.

Apartment from the pre-test, there were three sub-tests (mainly objective type) prepared by the investigator, these tests were given to the experts who have been teaching physics methods at various colleges of education for establishing content validity. As per the suggestions given by the experts the tests were further modified. Later, these tests were Brown prophecy formula. It was found to be 0.70, 0.79 respectively. These three sub-tests were administered periodically for both control and experimental group (after the completion of the corresponding sub programmes). The aggregate scores obtained by each trainee from all the three sub-tests and also the post-test given at the end constitute the achievement scores in physics. A copy of the tests are enclosed in Appendix.

Tool of Critical Thinking Skills (TOCTS)

The research has conducted a formal discussion meet with 30 experienced teachers to select the suitable components of critical thinking skills (using the 10 components given by Terry Applegate & Anitha Harnadek – 1987). In addition to this the researcher gave orientation to 30 B.Ed students regarding the different components of critical thinking skills. Later, they were given worksheets containing the sub units of the subject namely methods of teaching physics. They were instructed to identify the components of critical thinking skills under each sub unit.

Based on the suggestions made by the experts, experienced teachers and B.Ed trainees, the following six components of critical thinking skills were selected. Namely;

1. Determining the relevance of information.
2. Determining the factual accuracy of a statement.
3. Determining the credibility of a source.
4. Identifying the unstated assumptions.
5. Determining between verifiable facts from value claims.

Under each of the above component, 15 items were given to five experts for validation (content and contruct). Their suggestions were considered and the tool was further modified and refined.

Later the tool was tried out on a small group. Based on time validity only 36 items were finally selected and the average time required to complete the tool was found to be 60 minutes. To find the reliability co-efficient Spearman Brown Prophecy formula was used using the split half method. The reliability co-efficient was found to be 0.83. This tool was considered for the pre-test and keeping this test, a parallel test was also constructed, which was administered as post test.

Scoring Procedure for CTS Tool

For the components 1, 2, 3, 4 and 5 under each item the expected answer will be Most Relevant (MR) or Relevant (R) or Least Relevant (LR)

Weightage in Terms of Marks

Most Relevant (MR)	*Relevant (R)*	*Least Relevant (LR)*
3 marks	2 marks	1 mark

Where as for the component 6, the expected answer will be Only Facts, Only Opinion or Both Facts and Opinion.

Weightage in Terms of Marks

Only Facts	*Only Opinion*	*Both fact and opinion*
1 marks	1 marks	1 mark

If only Fact or Only Opinion is answered with reasoning, one additional mark will be added in both the cases.

Total Weightage of Marks for All the Components

1st component	(6 x 3)	= 18 marks
2nd component	(6 x 3)	= 18 marks
3rd component	(6 x 3)	= 18 marks
4th component	(6 x 3)	= 18 marks
5th component	(6 x 3)	= 18 marks
6th component	(6 x 5)	= 30 marks
Total		**120 marks**

Administration of the Tools

The above tools were administered to the B.Ed. trainees

who have taken methods of teaching physics and were studying in four different colleges of education.

Based on the scores of the creative thinking ability skills, using t-test (using mean and standard deviation) the trainees were divided into two groups namely – 'experimental' and 'control'.

Developing a Programme of Critical Thinking Skills (POCTS)

In the present the, the investigator has followed the subject matter approach to develop critical thinking skills. There are different programmes prepared commercially are available in other countries. (Edward De Bono's CORT, Sidney Parnes creative problem solving....etc.). These programmes have other limitations also. In addition to this, they are seldom on which they process by using the content drawn primarily from the life experiences of the students. There is no guarantee that most of the students have seriously shown concern towards those experiences. Therefore it is necessary to select the subject matter which is common for all the students, to develop the thinking skills programme. Thus the sub programmes were prepared keeping B.Ed. syllabus (methods of teaching Physics). The researcher has developed 16 sub programmes related to the six components of critical thinking skills. These sub programmes were validated with the experts who are teaching the subjects. As per their suggestions sub programmes were modified. The modified Programme was given as treatment to the experimental group for a period of three months (32) hours).

Stages involved in developing the Programme of Critical Thinking Skillks (POCTS).

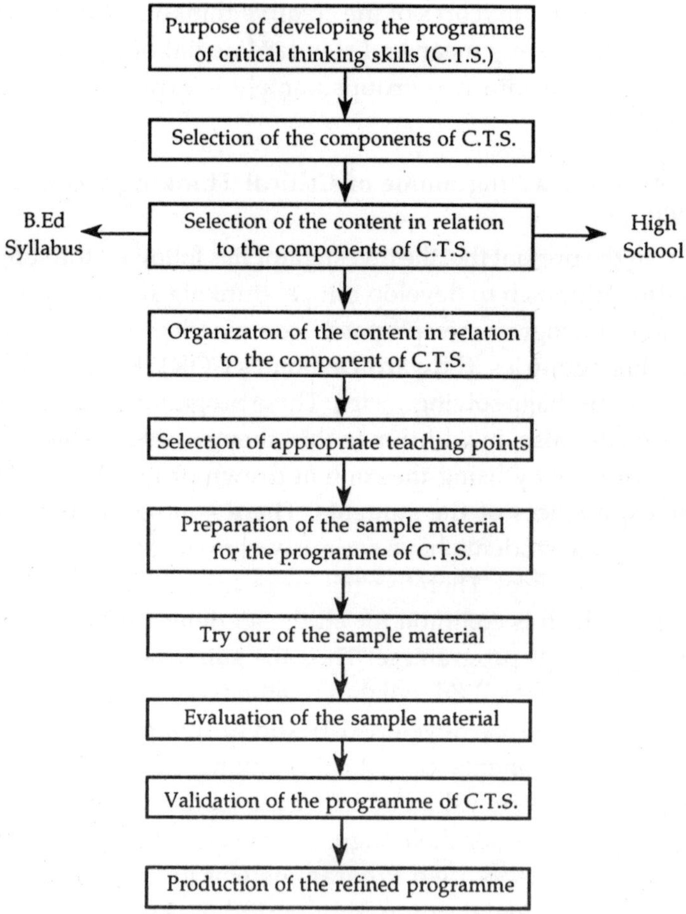

PHASE I

(a) Selection of the components of critical thinking skills. In order to identify the component of Critical thinking skills which can be fitted well under each sub unit, the suggestions made by the experts, experienced teachers and B.Ed trainees were considered. The 6 components of CTS selected for praying the Tool of Critical thinking Skills (TOCTS) among the 10 companies given by Terry Applegate and Anitha Harnade K (1987) to develop programme on CTS.

Berry K. Beyer (1988) has given the following guidelines in relation to different components of creative thinking skills.

1. *Determining the Relevance of Information*

Definition: Deciding whether something relates or pertains to the matter at hand.

Relevance: Pertaining or related to the subject matter.

Rules: a specific topic is the matter at hand- identifying the elements of a problem where there is a considerable amount of information.

2. *Determining the Accuracy of a Statement*

Definition: Determining whether or not a factual statement is true and consistent with other known facts.

Accuracy: Correctness, exactness, consistency with other known facts.

Rules: When using data or sources to solve problems or make decisions.

When factual statements are to be used to build generalization or similar kinds of knowledge claims.

Whenever someone is trying to persuade or convince about something.

3. *Determining the Credibility of a Source*

Definition: Deciding whether a source is believable, in terms of credibility, and reliability.

Rules: In determining the accuracy of information or claims in another source. In collection for use in a task.

4. Identifying the Unstated Assumption

Definition: Identifying an unstated premise or ascertain that must be presumed or accepted as true if that which is stated is to be considered true.

Assumption: Presumption, supposition something taken for granted. Rules:

(a) In determining the strength of an argument.

(b) Some one is trying to prove that something is true.

In trying to determine the accuracy or validity of a claim or conclusion..

(c) In trying to learn about an author's point of view.

5. Identifying the Strength of an Argument

Definition: Identifying the parts of an argument.

Argument: A justified position reasons given in support of a conclusion. Deciding the quality or merit of reasons given in support of a conclusion.

Strength: Quality, merit, believability.

Argument: Reasons given in support of a conclusion.

Rules: Any time some one is trying to convince or persuade some one about the truth, accuracy, or durability of something. – any time someone is trying to determine the validity of any conclusion.

6. Distinguishing between Verifiable Facts from Value Claim

Definition: Separating statements about things that have been proven or could be objectively proven from statements that cannot be objectively proven to everyone's satisfaction.

Fact: Objectively proven or capable of being objectively proven.

Value Claim: a subjective determination about the worth of something.

Rules: In determining the accuracy of a report other account. In determining the strength of an argument.

The researcher has discussed the sub-units which come under the methods of teaching physics, with the experts. The thorough open discussion with the experts helped him in identifying the suitable sub-units as per the components of CTS.

Development of the programme of critical thinking skills using the sub units of the methods of teaching physics.

Each sub-programme usually contains two aspects namely.

1. Description part and
2. Exercise part

The description part contains an episode or a problem or an experiment, whereas the exercise part contains Yes/No type questions seeking for reasoning along with a few short answer type of questions. These sub-programmes were given to experts to collect their opinion and suggestions regarding the content validity.

The 16 sub-programmes developed were tried out on a small group of B.Ed. trainees. As per the opinion of the experts and also on basis of the feedback obtained by the try-out group the sub-programmes were further modified. The try-out also helped the researcher to structure the programme in terms of instruction, time schedule, description and evaluation. Thus the 16 sub programmes of CTS were refined based on the feedback from the try out and pilot study.

PHASE II

Implementation of the programme of critical thinking skills (POCTS)

(a) Formation of Small Groups

The experimental group (methods of teaching Physics) was further sub-divided into smaller groups, randomly. The size of the small group was limited to five to six trainees. In each small group, there was a leader who moderated the group discussion.

(b) Procedure Involved in Administering the Sub-Programmes

In the first stage, the researcher, after forming the smaller group, distributed the sub programme sheets to all the trainees. They were asked to read the sheet as per the direction, and answer the questions which come under it. After giving sufficient time for answering the sheets, they were collected back. In the second stage, the same content was discussed in small groups. Each group arrived at some common answers related to the questions of the sub-programme. Thereby the questions which were difficult to answer at the individual level were given opportunity to present the group report for the benefit of the entire group. During this time other students were permitted to react and clarify their doubts. In the final stage, after clarifying the doubts, the investigator concluded the discussion. In this way the same procedure was followed to complete all the 16 sub-programmes. Where programmes involved the use of transparencies, work-books, resources units and experiments, the each individual was allowed to see, read or perform the experiment followed by the group participation.

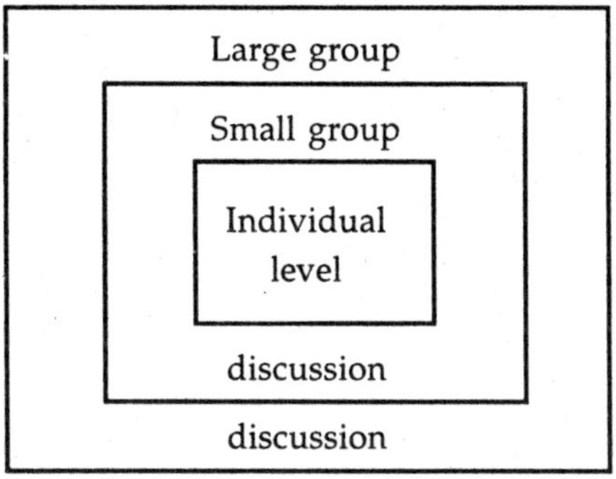

Figure 4. the stucture of the group discussion.

Example: Sub programme 6

Inquiry Skills

Instructions: Read the following passage and answer the questions given below.

EXPERIMENTAL SITUATION: BELL JAR EXPERIMENT

A teacher was conducting the bell jar experiment to prove that sound does not travel in vaccum. He described the apparatus to the students. Later he instructed the students that when the air in the bell jar was taken out gradually with the help of an exhaust/vaccum pump, the sound produced by the electric bell will be diminished. Wheen all the students were observing the experiment keenly, though the air was removed gradually the bell was producing the same intensity of sounds as before. Teacher was surprised and faced with the question, why the intensity of sound of the bell did not decrease when the air in the bell jar is removed gradually?

Exercise

1. What is the problem faced by the teacher?
2. Write the possible causes due to which the intensity of the sound of the electric bell did not decrease.

3. Rearrange the cause in terms of more relevant to least relevant cause.
4. Write the reasons to explain how each one is a cause.
5. Identify certain assumptions on your own and on this basis find out the probable cause for the problem.

The above sheet was given to every trainee and asked to answer the questions given under the exercise. Later, the answers written by each trainee was discussed in small group to clarify their doubts. The report prepared by each group was presented in a large group for further clarification and better understanding. The investigation at this stage clarified their doubts arising out of different groups discussions.

(c) Administration of the Test

After completing the first 4 sub programmes, a formative test was administered. Similarly after the completion of the 2nd and 3rd set of programmes (sub-programmes5-10 & 11-16 respectively) similar formative tests were given. And at the end of the completion of all the 16 sub-programmes, a final test was administered.

The performance of the trainees in all the sub-programmes as per the different components of CTS were tested and ascertained their improvement in all the components.

Details Regarding the Input of POCTS

The 16 sub-programmes develoed by the researcher was carried on for a period of 32 hours (approx.) for the experimental group.

TABLE 3.1

Area of the Sub-Programme, Time Allotted for Recording the Thoughts, Time Allotted fro Discussion, No. of Questions, Components Covered and the Percentage of Weightage Given to the Components

Sub Prog-ramme	*Area Unit*	*Time for recording the thought*	*Time of Discussion recording*	*No. of Ques-tions*	*Components Covered*	*Weigh-tage %*
1.	Meaning & Nature of Science	15 Min	30 Min	4	C1,C2	35%
2.	Concepts & Principles	20 Min	40 Min	9	C1,C2, C3, C5, C6	85%
3.	Scientific method	30 Min	60 Min	5	C1, C2, C5, C6	65%
4.	Scientific attitude					
	A. Classroom situations	10 MIn	45 Min	6	C2, C3, C4, C5	65%
	B. Scientific attitude questionnaire	15 Min	60 Min	16	C1, C2, C4, C5, C6	85%
	C. General episodes	20 Min	30 Minutes	4	C2, C4, C5, C6	65%
5.	Inductive & deductive approaches	40 Minutes	80 Minutes	7	C1, C2, C3, C5, C6	85%
6.	Inquiry skills					
	A. Electrolysis					
	B. Bell Jar expt					
	C. Discharge tube	45 Min	45 + 90 Min	6	C1, C2, C3, C4, C5, C6	85%
	D. Convention					
	E. Properties of magnets					
7.	Problem Solving					
	A. Bending of candle flame					
	B. Spraying of water					
	C. Ping pong ball	45 Min.	45 + 90 Min	5	C1, C2, C3, C5, C6	70%
	D. Electro magentic induction					
	E. Floating of cork					
8.	Models					
	A. Expansion of gases					
	B. Telescope/ microscope					

contd...

Sub Prog-ramme	*Area Unit*	*Time for recording the thought*	*Time of Discussion recording*	*No. of Ques-tions*	*Components Covered*	*Weigh-tage %*
	C. Transformer	45 MIn	45 + 60 Min	7	C1, C2, C3, C5, C6	85%
	D. Black body radiation					
	E. Electric motor					
9.	Resource unit-modern physics					
10.	Transparancies					
	A. Optical Instruments	45 Min	45 + 45 Min	7	C1, C3, C4, C5, C6	85%
	B. Spherical mirrors					
11.	Science club activities	30 Min	60 + 30 Min	7	C1, C5	35%
12.	Field trips	30 Min	60 + 30 Min	6	C1, C5	35%
13.	Science magazine	30 Min	60 Min	7	C1, C2, C3, C5, C6	85%
14.	Unit test					
	A. Short answer	20 Min	50 Min	10	C1, C3, C5	65%
	B. Multiple choice	20 Min		10	C6	
15.	Reasoning test					
	A. Observation	45 Min	75 Min		25	
	B. Brain stroming					
	A.. 1. Energy					
	2. Source of energy					
	3. Petroleum					
	4. Solar energy					
	5. Water pollution					
	6. Air pollution					
	B. 1. Uses of dry cell	10 Min	50 Min	3	C1, C2, C3, C5	75%
	2. Usesof tuning fork					
	3. Uses of lense					
	4. Uses of bulbs					
	5. Spring balance					
	6. Spherical mirrors					

Design of the Research

The present study involves experimental design wherein factorial design is considered for analysis of the data.

Experimental Design

While determining the experiment for study the researcher

has kept the following characteristics of a well designed experiment (Robert. M.W. Travers).

While discussion the experimental design experts use two terms namely pre-test and post-test in connection with data collection. Pre-test consists the measure or test given to the subjects prior to the experimental treatment. A post-test is a measure given after the experimental treatment has been completed.

Experimental design usually involves 2 groups namely the experimental and control group. The treatment will be given to the experimental group. In the present study, the researchers has followed two group design. It can be diagramatically shown as follow.

Control Group	Experimental Group
Pre-test (T.O.C.T.S. and Achievement)	**Pre-test** (T.O.C.T.S. and Achievement)
*Content Treatment	Content Treatment and Programme of critical thinking skills
Post-test (T.O.C.T.S. and Achievement)	**Post-test** (T.O.C.T.S. and Achievement)

*Content treatment is through structured lectures – 16 hours from August to September

Procedure Adopted in Equating the Froup Matching

In the present study the selection of the two groups consists of assigning subjects to experimental and control groups in such a way that, the means and the variances of the groups on initial test of critical thinking skills are as nearly equal as possible. (Experimental group X = 75.91; s = 10.1; Control group X = 73.4; s = 8.13).

Factorial Design

The essential principle that R.A. Fisher introduced to revolutionize experimental design was the concept that more than one factor could be varied within the structure of a single experiment. Such as experiment involving many factors may contain all the information and provide the same precision as a series of independent experiments involving each of the factors singly, and it will provide savings in effort and work on the part of the experimenter. An additional advantage of the multifactor design is that it may permit the estimation of the effect of the interaction of the variables.

A factorial design comprises the basic construction of a design in which all levels of each independent variable taken in the combination with levels of the other independent variables (Allen). A factorial design requires a minimum of two independent variables with at least two levels of variables. This minimum design is called a two-by-two (2 x 2) factorial. This design helps in finding out the main interaction methods among the variables. In the present study there are four variables namely sex, SES, intelligence and critical thinking skills. Each variable is varied at two levels namely high and low using median as a cut off point. Hence the study involves (2 x 2 x 2 x 2) factorial design.

Variance main effects	*Source of variance*	*Degree of freedom*
A	Sex	1
B	SES	1
C	Intelligence(In t)	1
D	Critical thinking skills (CTS)	1
Two way interaction		
A x B	Sex x SES	1
A x C	Sex x Int	1
A x D	Sex x CTS	1
B x C	Sex x Int	1

Variance main effects	Source of variance	Degree of freedom
B x D	Sex x CTS	1
C x D	Int x CTS	1
Three way interaction		
A x B x C	Sex x SES x Int	1
A x C x D	Sex x Int x CTS	1
B x C x D	SES x Int x CTS	1
B x D x A	SES x Int x Sex	1
Four way interaction		
A x B x C x D	Sex x SES x Int x CTS	1

Statistical Tools

In the present study, a 4-way analysis of variance, t-test and percentile ranks were used to analyse the data.

The 4-way analysis of variance has been used to analyse the data in terms of main and interaction effects (2 x 2 x 2 x 2 factorial design).

The t-test has been used to compare the significant difference between the means of pre-test and post-test scores of creative thinking skills.

Percentile ranks were used to compare the performance of trainees regarding the different components of the Programme of Critical Thinking Skills (POCTS).

In addition to the above tools, correlation technique has also been used to find the inter correlation among the components of critical thinking.

So far, the researcher has discussed the methodology adopted for the study. In the next chapter the researcher deals with the analysis of the data based on the statistical tools.

4

ANALYSIS AND INTERPRETATION

In the previous chapter, the methodology adopted for the present study was discussed in detail, where as this chapter deals with analysis and interpretation of the data.

As stated earlier the main purpose of the investigation was to find out the impact of the programme of Critical thinking skills on the achievement of secondary school teacher trainees, major and minor hypotheses have been formulated as mentioned in the previous chapter. each one of these hypotheses was tested using the Analysis of Variance and test.

MAJOR HYPOTHESES 1

There is no significant difference between the pre test and post test mean scores of experimental and control group regarding Critical thinking skills based on achievement in methods of teaching physics.

Hypotheses 1.1

There is no significant difference between the pre test and post test mean scores of achievement in methods of teaching physics of experimental and control group regarding the component of Critical thinking skills namely determining the relevance of information.

TABLE 4.1

Source of Variation, Sum of Squares, Degrees of Freedom, Mean Squares, the Value of F and its Significance of Pre Test and Post Test Scores of Experimental and Control Group Regarding the Component of Critical Thinking Skills Namely Determining the Relevance of Information

Source of variation	*Sum of squares*	*DF*	*Mean square*	*F*	*Significance of F*
Explained (between groups)	3,000	1	3,000	1.085	
Residual (within groups)	293,000	106	2,764		
Total	296,00	107	2,766		NS

(NS = NON Significant, S =Significant,
S* = Significant at 0.05 level, S**= Significant at 00.01 level.)

Hypothesis 1.1 a

There is no significant difference between the pre test and post test mean scores of achievements in methods of teaching physics based on critical thinking skill (after the implementation of the programme of Critical thinking skills.) among the teacher trainees of the experimental group.

TABLE 4.1 A

Nature of Tests, Means Scores, Standard Deviation, t-Value and its Significance in Achievement in Methods of Teaching Physics Based on Critical Thinking Skills of the Experimental Group

Nature of Test	*N*	*Mean Scores*	*Standard deviation*	*t-Value of the t*	*Significance*
Pre-Test	55	83.9454	13,86592	9,38302	S
Post-Test	55	110.16364	15.400		

Since the computed value of 'the null hypothesis is rejected. This means that there is significant difference in the achievement in methods of teaching physics based on Critical thinking skills, after the completion of the programme of Critical thinking skills.

Hypothesis 1.1.b

There is no significant difference between the post test mean scores of the control group and experimental group teacher trainees regarding achievement in methods of teaching physics based on Critical thinking skills.

TABLE 4.1-B

Nature of Test Mean Scores Standard Deviation t-Value and its Significance in Achievement in Methods of Teaching Physics Based on the Critical Thinking Skills of Control and Experimental Group

Nature of Test	*N*	*Mean Scores*	*Standard deviation*	*t-Value of the t*	*Significance*
Pre-Test (Control)	55	102.13636	16.5185	2.736	S
Post Test (Control)	55	110.16364	15.400		

Since the computed value of 't' if greater than the table value of 't' the null hypothesis is rejected. This means that there is significant difference in the achievement in methods of teaching physics based on CTS among the teacher trainees of control and experimental group.

From the above table it is evident that the computer valueof 'F' is less than the table value (3.92 at 0.05 level). Hence it is not significant. Therefore the null hypothesis was accepted. This means that there is no significant difference between the pre test and post test scores of achievement in methods of teaching physics of experimental and control group regarding the components of critical thinking skills namely determining the relevance of information.

Hypothesis 1.2

There is no significant difference between the pre test and post test mean scores of achievement in methods of teaching physics of experimental and control group regarding the component of Critical thinking skills namely determining the accuracy of factual claim.

TABLE 4.2

Source of Variation, Sum of Square Degrees of Freedom, Mean Squares, the Value of F and its Significance of Pre Test and Post Test Scores of the Experimental and Control Group Regarding the Component of Critical Thinking Skills Namely Determining the Accuracy of Factual Claim

Source of variation	*Sum of squares*	*DF*	*Mean square*	*F*	*Significance of F*
Explained (between groups)	0.009	1	0.009	0.0020	
Residual (within groups)	502.907	106	4.744		
Total	502.927	107	4.700		NS

Since the computed value of 'F' is less than table value of 'F, the null hypothesis was accepted. This means that there is no significant difference between the pre test and post test scores of achievement in methods of teaching physics of experimental and control group regarding the component of Critical thinking skills namely determining the accuracy of factual claim.

Hypothesis 1.3

There is no significant difference between the pre test and post test mean scores of achievement in methods of teaching physics of experimental and control groups regarding the component of critical thinking skills namely determining credibility of a source.

TABLE 4.3

Source of Variation, Sum of Squares, Degrees of Freedom, Mean Squares, the Value of F and its Significance of Pre Test and Post Test Scores of the Experimental and Control of Group Regarding the Component of Critical Thinking Skills Namely Determining the Credibility of a Source

Source of variation	*Sum of squares*	*DF*	*Mean square*	*F*	*Significance of F*
Explained (between groups)	118.231	1	118.231	1.085	
Residual (within groups)	287.204	106	2.709		S**
Total	405.435	107	2.789		

Since the computed value of 'F' is more than the table of F (at0.01 level) the null hypothesis was rejected. This means that there is a significant difference between the pre test and post test mean scores of achievement in methods of teaching physics of the experimental and control group regarding the component of critical thinking skills namely determining the credibility of a source.

Hypothesis 1.4

There is no significant difference between the pre test and post test mean scores of achievement in methods of teaching physics of experimental and control group regarding the component of critical thinking skills namely identifying the unstated assumption.

Since the computed value of 'F' is more than the table value of 'F',(at 0.01 level) null hypothesis was rejected. This means that there is significant difference between the pre test and pot test mean scores of achievement in methods of teaching physics of the control group regarding the component of critical thinking skills namely distinguishing statement of fact from value claim.

TABLE 4.4

Source of Variation, Sum of Squares, Degrees of Freedom, Mean Squares, the Value of F and its Significance of Pre Test and Post Test Scores of Experimental and Control Group Regarding the Component of Critical Thinking Skills Namely Identifying the Unstated Assumption

Source of variation	*Sum of squares*	*DF*	*Mean square*	*F*	*Significance of F*
Explained (between groups)	355.704	1	355.704	32.9510	
Residual (within groups)	1144.259	106	10.795		
Total	1499.963	107	14.018		S**

From the above table it is evident that the obtained value of 'F' is more than the table value of 'F; (at 0.01 level). Hence the null hypothesis was rejected. This means that there is a significant difference between the pre test and post test mean scores of achievement in methods of teaching physics of experimental and control group regarding the component of critical thinking skills namely identifying the unstated assumption.

Hypothesis 1.5

There is no significant difference between the pre test and post mean scores of achievement in methods of teaching physics of experimental and control group regarding the component of critical thinking skills namely determining the strength of an argument.

From the above table it is evident that the obtained value of 'F' is more than the table value of 'F' (6.85 at 0.0evel). hence the null hypothesis was rejected. This means that there is a significant difference between the pre test and post test mean scores of achievement in methods of teaching physics of experimental and control group regarding the component of critical thinking skills namely determining the strength of an argument.

TABLE 4.5

Source of Variation, Sum of Squares, Degrees of Freedom, Mean Squares, the Value of F and its Significance of Pre Test and Post Test Scores of Experimental and Control Group Regarding the Component of Critical Thinking Skills Namely Determining the Strength of an Argument

Source of variation	*Sum of squares*	*DF*	*Mean square*	*F*	*Significance of F*
Explained (between groups)	104.037	1	104.037	5.424	
Residual (within groups)	293,000	106	19.181		
Total	296,00	107	19.974		S*

Hypothesis 1.6

There is no significant difference between the pre test and post test mean scores of achievement in methods of teaching physics of experimental and control group regarding the component of critical thinking skills namely distinguishing statement of fact from value judgment.

TABLE 4.6

Source of Variation, Sum of Squares, Degrees of Freedom, Mean Squares, the Value of F and its Significance of Pre Test and Post Test Scores of Experimental and Control Group Regarding the Components of Critical Thinking Skills Namely Distinguishing Statement of Fact from Value Judgement

Source of variation	*Sum of squares*	*DF*	*Mean square*	*F*	*Significance of F*
Explained	341.333	1	341.333	18.487	S**
Residual	1957.074				
Total	2298.407				

Hypothesis 1.7

There is no significant difference between the pre test and post test mean scores of achievement in methods of teaching physics of experimental and control group regarding all the components of critical thinking skill.

TABLE 4.7

Source of Variation, Sum of Squares, Degrees of Freedom, Mean Squares, the Value of F and its Significance of Pre Test and Post Test Scores of Experimental and Control Group Regarding All the Components of Critical Thinking Skills

Source of variation	*Sum of squares*	*DF*	*Mean square*	*F*	*Significance of F*
Explained (between groups)	3524.898	1	3524.898	36.677	
Residual (within groups)	10187.352	106	96.107		S
Total	13712.250	107	128.152		

Since the computed value of 'F' is more than the table value of 'F' (at 0.01 level), the null hypothesis was rejected. This means that there is a significant difference between the pre test post mean scores of achievement in methods of teaching physics of experimental and control group regarding all the components of critical thinking skill.

Further, it indicates that, there is no significant difference between the pre test and post test scores of achievement in methods of teaching physics of the experimental and control group with respect to the components namely determining the relevance of information and determining the factual accuracy of a claim.

MAJOR HYPOTHESIS 2

There is no significant difference between pre test and post test mean scores of control group regarding critical thinking skills based on achievement in methods of teaching physics.

Hypothesis 2.1

There is no significant difference between pre test and post test mean scores of achievement in methods of teaching physics of control group regarding the component of critical thinking skills namely determining the relevance of information.

TABLE 4.8

Source of Variation, Sum of Squares, Degrees of Freedom, Mean Squares, the Value of F and its Significance of Pre Test and Post Test Scores of Control Group Regarding the Component of Critical Thinking Skills Namely Determining the Relevance of Information

Source of variation	*Sum of squares*	*DF*	*Mean square*	*F*	*Significance of F*
Explained	0.926	1	0.926	0.236	
Residual	415.259	106	3.918		
Total	416.185	107	3.890		NS

Since the computed value of 'F' is less than table value of 'F', the null hypothesis was accepted. This means that there is no significant difference between the pre test and post test mean scores of achievement in methods of teaching physics of control group regarding the component of critical thinking skills namely determining the relevance of information.

Hypothesis 2.2

There is no significant difference between pre test and post test mean scores of achievement in methods of teaching physics of control group regarding the component of critical thinking skills namely determining the accuracy of factual claim.

TABLE 4.9

Source of Variation, Sum of Squares, Degrees of Freedom, Mean Squares, the Value of F and its Significance of Pre Test and Post Test Scores of Control Group Regarding the Component of Critical Thinking Skills Namely Determining the Accuracy of Factual Claim

Source of variation	*Sum of squares*	*DF*	*Mean square*	*F*	*Significance of F*
Explained	0.231	1	0.231	0.076	
Residual	322.315	106	3.041		
Total	322.546	107	3.041		NS

Since the computed value of 'F' is less than the table value o 'F' ,the null hypothesis was accepted. This means that there is no significant difference between the pre test and post test mean scores of achievement in methods of teaching physics of control group regarding the component of critical thinking skills namely determining the accuracy of factual claim.

Hypothesis 2.3

There is no significant difference between pre test and post test mean scores of achievement in methods of teaching physics of control group regarding the component of critical thinking skills namely determining the credibility of a source.

Since the computed value of 'F' is more than the table value of 'F' (at 0.05 level), the null hypothesis was rejected. This means that there is a significant difference between the pre test and post test mean scores of achievement in methods of teaching physics of control group regarding the component of critical thinking skills namely determining the credibility of a source.

TABLE 4.10

Source of Variation, Sum of Squares, Degrees of Freedom, Mean Squares, the Value of F and its Significance of Pre Test and Post Test Scores of Control Group Regarding the Component of Critical Thinking Skills Namely Determining the Credibility 1 of a Source

Source of variation	*Sum of squares*	*DF*	*Mean square*	*F*	*Significance of F*
Explained	23.148	1	23.146	6.693	
Residual	366.593	106	3.450		
Total	389.741	107	3.642		S**

Hypothesis 2.4

There is no significant difference between pre test and post test mean scores of achievement in methods of teaching physics of control group regarding the component of critical thinking skill namely identifying the unstated assumption.

TABLE 4.11

Source of Variation, Sum of Squares, Degrees of Freedom, Mean Squares, the Value of F and its Significance of Pre Test and Post Test Scores of Control Group Regarding the Component of Critical Thinking Skills Namely Identifying the Unstated Assumption

Source of variation	*Sum of squares*	*DF*	*Mean square*	*F*	*Significance of F*
Explained	102.083	1	102.083	7.023	
Residual	1540.685	106	24.535		
Total	1642.769	107	15.353		S**

From the above table it is evident that the obtained value of 'F' is more than the table value of 'F' (at 0.01 level), the null hypothesis was rejected. This means that there is significant difference between the pre test and post test mean scores of the unstated assumption.

Hypothesis 2.5

There is no significant difference between pre test and post test mean scores of achievement in methods of teaching physics of control group regarding the component of critical thinking skills namely determining the strength of an argument.

TABLE 4.12

Source of Variation, Sum of Squares, Degrees of Freedom, Mean Squares, the Value of F and its Significance of Pre Test and Post Test Scores of Control Group Regarding the Component of Critical Thinking Skills Namely Determining the Strength of an Argument

Source of variation	*Sum of squares*	*DF*	*Mean square*	*F*	*Significance of F*
Explained	56.333	1	56.333	1.865	
Residual	3201.852	106	30.206		
Total	3201.85	107	30.450		NS

Since the computed value of 'F' is less than the table value of 'F', the null hypothesis was accepted . This means that there is no significant difference between the pre test and post test mean scores of achievement in methods of teaching physics of control group regarding the component of critical thinking skills namely determining the strength of a argument.

Hypothesis 2.6

There is no significant difference between pre test and post test mean scores of achievement in methods of teaching physics of control group regarding the component of critical thinking skills namely distinguishing statement of fact from value judgment.

Table 4.13

Source of Variation, Sum of Squares, Degrees of Freedom, Mean Squares, the Value of F and its Significance of Pre Test and Post Test Scores of Control Group Regarding the Component of Critical Thinking Skills Namely Determining the Strength of the Fact from Value Judgement

Source of variation	*Sum of squares*	*DF*	*Mean square*	*F*	*Significance of F*
Explained	39.120	1	39.120	1.138	
Residual	3145.796	106	29.677		
Total	3184.3917	107	29.766		NS

Since the computed value of 'F' is less than the table value of 'F' the null hypothesis was accepted. This means that there is no significant difference between the pre test and post test mean scores of achievement in methods of teaching physics of control group regarding the component of critical thinking skills namely distinguishing statement of fact from value judgement.

Hypothesis 2.7

There is no significant difference between pre test and post test mean scores of achievement in methods of teaching physics of control group regarding all the components of critical thinking skills.

Since the computed value of 'F' is less than the table value of 'F', the null hypothesis was accepted. This means that there is not significant difference between the pre test and post test mean scores of achievement in methods of teaching physics of control group regarding all the components of critical thinking skills.

TABLE 4.14

Source of Variation, Sum of Squares, Degrees of Freedom, Mean Squares, the Value of F and its Significance of Pre Test and Post Test Scores of Control Group Regarding All the Components of the Critical Thinking Skills

Source of variation	*Sum of squares*	*DF*	*Mean square*	*F*	*Significance of F*
Explained	49.343	1	49.343	0.195	
Residual	26766.759	106	252.517		
Total	26816.102	107	250.618		NS

However, the analysis also indicates that there is significant difference between pre test and post test scores of achievement in methods o teaching physics of the control group with respect to the component namely determining the credibility of a source and identifying unstated assumption.

MAJOR HYPOTHESIS 3

There is not significant difference between the pre test mean scores of the experimental group and post test mean scores of the control group regarding critical thinking skills based on achievement in methods of teaching physiics.

Hypothesis 3.1

There is no significant difference between the pre test mean scores of the achievement in methods of teaching physics of experimental group and post test mean scores of the control group regarding the critical thinking skills namely determining the relevance of information.

Since the computed value of 'F' is less than the table value of 'F', the null hypothesis was accepted. This means that there is no significant difference between the pre test mean scores of the experimental group and post test mean scores of achievement in methods of teaching physics of control group regarding the component of critical thinking skills namely determining the relevance of information.

TABLE 4.15

Source of Variation, Sum of Squares, Degrees of Freedom, Mean Squares, the Value of F and its Pre Test Mean Scores of the Experimental Group and Post Test Mean Scores of the Control Froup Regarding the Component of Critical Thinking Skills Namely Determining the Relevance of Information

Source of variation	*Sum of squares*	*DF*	*Mean square*	*F*	*Significance of F*
Explained	15.500	3	5.167	1.547	
Residual	708.259	212	3.341		NS
Total	723.759	215	3.366		

Hypothesis 3.2

There is no significant difference between the pre test mean scores of the achievement in methods of teaching physics of experimental group and post test mean scores of the control group regarding the component of critical thinking skills namely determining the accuracy of factual claim.

TABLE 4.16

Source of Variation, Sum of Squares, Degrees of Freedom, Mean Squares, the Value o F and Its Significance of Pre Test Mean Scores of the Experimental Group and Post Test Mean Scores of the Control Group Regarding the Component of Critical Thinking Skills Namely Determining the Accuracy Factual Claim

Source of variation	*Sum of squares*	*DF*	*Mean square*	*F*	*Significance of F*
Explained	1.148	3	0.3836	0.098	
Residual	823.122	212	3.895		NS
Total	826.370	215	3.844		

Since the computed value of' F' is less than the table

value of"F' the null hypothesis was accepted. This means that there is no significant difference between the pre test mean scores of achievement in methods of teaching physics of the Experimental group and post test mean scores of the control group regarding the component of critical thinking skills namely determining the accuracy of factual claim.

Hypothesis 3.3

There is no significant difference between the pre test mean scores of the achievement in methods of teaching physics of experimental group and post test mean scores of the critical thinking skills namely determining the credibility of a source.

TABLE 4.17

Source of Variation, Sum of Squares, Degrees of Freedom, Mean Squares, the Value of F and the Its Significance of Pre Test Mean Scores of the Experimental Group and Post Test Mean Scores of the Control Group Regarding the Component of Critical Thinking Skills Namely Determining the Credibility of a Source

Source of variation	*Sum of squares*	*DF*	*Mean square*	*F*	*Significance of F*
Explained	142.162	3	47.387	15.266	
Residual	653.796	212	3.084		S**
Total	795.958	215	3.702		

Since the computed value of 'F' is greater than the table value of 'F' (at 0.01 level), the null hypothesis was rejected. This means that there is a significant difference between the pre test mean scores of achievement in methods of teaching physics of the experimental group and post test mean scores of the control group regarding the component of critical thinking skills namely determining the credibility of a source.

Hypothesis 3.4

There is no significant difference between the pre test mean scores of the achievement in methods of teaching physics of experimental group and post test mean scores of the control group regarding the component of critical thinking skills namely identifying the unstated assumptions.

TABLE 4.18

Source of Variation, Sum of Squares, Degrees of Freedom, Mean Squares, the Value of F and its Significance of Pre Test Mean Scores of the Experimental Group and Post Test Mean Scores of the Control Group Regarding the Component of Critical Thinking Skills Namely Identifying the Unstated Assumption

Source of variation	*Sum of squares*	*DF*	*Mean square*	*F*	*Significance of F*
Explained	468.014	3	156.005	12.318	
Residual	2684.944	212	29.677		S**
Total	3152.958	215	29.766		

Since the computed value of 'F' is greater than the table value of 'F' (at 0.01level), the null hypothesis was rejected. This means that there is significant difference between the pre test mean scores of achievement in methods of teaching physics of the experimental group and post test mean scores of the control group regarding the component of the critical thinking skills namely identifying the unstated assumption.

Hypothesis 3.5

There is no significant difference between the pre test mean scores of the experimental group and post test mean scores of achievement in methods of teaching physics of the control group regarding the component of critical thinking skills namely determining the strength of an argument.

TABLE 4.19

Source of Variation, Sum of Squares, Degrees of Freedom, Mean Squares, the Value of F and Its Significance of Pre Test Mean Scores of the Experimental Group and Post Test Mean Scores of the Control Froup Regarding the Control Froup Regarding the Component of Critical Thinking Skills Namely Determining the Strength of an Argument

Source of variation	*Sum of squares*	*DF*	*Mean square*	*F*	*Significance of F*
Explained	163.500	3	54.500	2.207	
Residual	5235.000	212	24.693		NS
Total	5398.500	215	25.109		

Since the computed value of 'F' is less than the table value of 'F' (at 0.01 level), the null hypothesis was accepted. This means that there is no significant difference between the pre test means scores of achievement in methods of teaching physics of the experimental group and post test mean scores of the control group regarding the component of the critical thinking skills namely determining the strength of an argument.

Hypothesis 3.6

There is no significant difference between the pre test mean scores of the experimental group and post test mean scores of achievement in methods of teaching physics of the control group regarding the component of critical thinking skills namely distinguishing statement of fact from value judgment.

Since the computed value of 'F' is great than the table value of 'F' (at 0.01 level), the null hypothesis was rejected. This means that there is a significant difference between the pre test mean scores of achievement in methods of teaching physics of the experimental group and post test mean scores of the control group regarding the component of the critical thinking skills namely distinguishing statement of fact from value judgment.

TABLE 4.20

Source of Variation, Sum of Squares, Degrees of Freedom, Mean Squares, the Value of F and Its Significance of Pre Test Mean Scores of the Experimental Group and Post Test Mean Scores of the Control Group Regarding the Control Group Regarding the Component of Critical Thinking Skills Namely Distinguishing Statement of Fact from Value Judgement

Source of variation	*Sum of squares*	*DF*	*Mean square*	*F*	*Significance of F*
Explained	963.903	3	321.301	13.349	
Residual	5120.870	212	24.070		
Total	6066.773	215	28.210		S*

Hypothesis 3.7

There is no significant difference between the pre test mean scores of the achievement in methods of teaching physics of experimental group and post test means scores of the control group regarding all components of critical thinking skills.

TABLE 4.21

Source of Variation, Sum of Squares, Degrees of Freedom, Mean Squares, the Value of F and its Significance of Pre Test Mean Scores of the Experimental Group and Post Test Mean Scores of the Control Group Regarding the Control Group Regarding All the Components of Critical Thinking Skills

Source of variation	*Sum of squares*	*DF*	*Mean square*	*F*	*Significance of F*
Explained	4352.481	3	1450.827	8.323	
Residual	36954.111	212	174.312		S**
Total	41036.593	215	192.124		

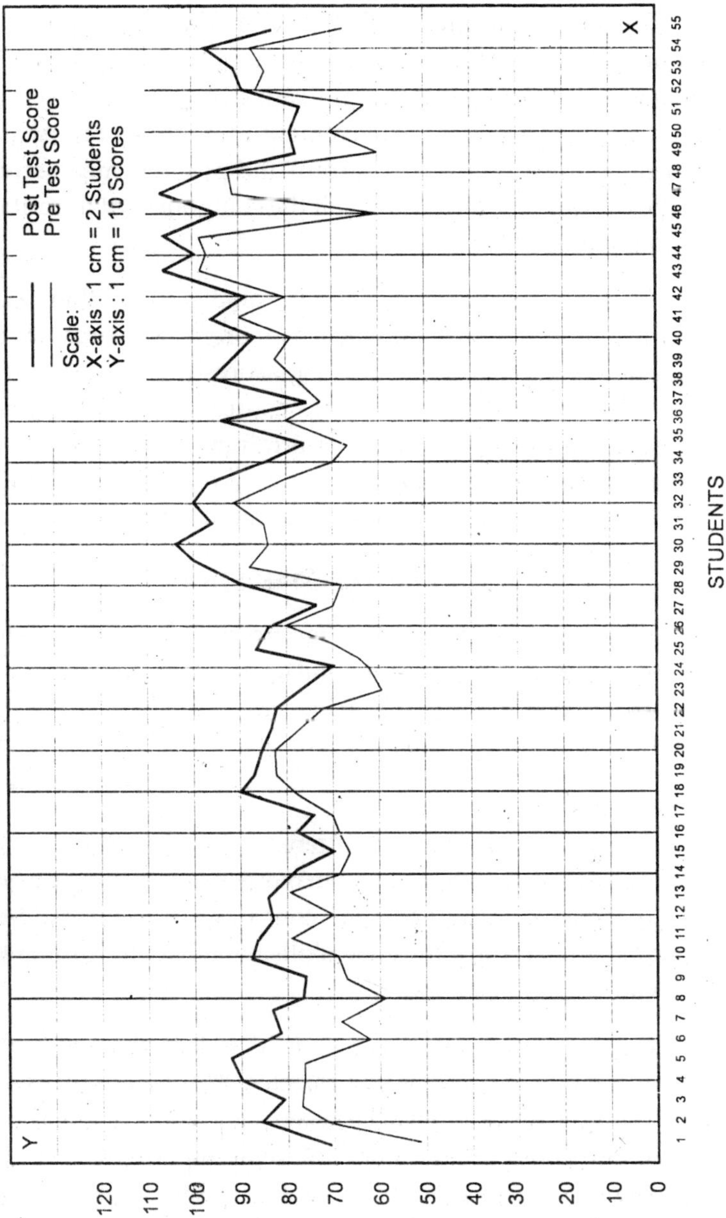

The mean critical thinking scores obtained by the experimental group. [pre & post test total scores]

Since the computed value of 'F' is great than the table value of 'F' (at 0.01 level), the null hypothesis was rejected. This means that there is a significant difference between the pre test mean scores of achievement in methods of teaching physics of the experimental group and post test mean scores of the control group regarding all the component of the critical thinking skills.

Further, it is very clear from the analysis that, there is no significant difference between the pre test scores of the experimental group and post test scores of achievement in methods of teaching physics of the control group with respect to the components namely determining the relevance of information, determining the accuracy of factual claim and determining the strength of an argument.

MAJOR HYPOTHESIS 4

There is no significant difference between the pre test mean scores of the experimental group and control group regarding critical thinking skills based on achievement in methods of teaching physics.

Hypothesis 4.1

There is no significant difference between the pre test mean scores of the achievement in methods of teaching physics of experimental group and the control group regarding the component of critical thinking skills namely determining the relevance of information.

Since the computed value of 't' is less than the table value, the null hypothesis was rejected. This means that there is no significant difference between the pre test mean scores of achievement in methods of teaching physics of the experimental group and the control group regarding the component of the critical thinking skills namely determining the relevance of information.

TABLE 4.22

Number of Cases, Standard Deviation, Standard Error, t-Value and a Significance of t of Post Test Mean Scores of the Experimental Group and Control Group Regarding the Control Group Regarding the Component of Critical Thinking Skills Namely Determining the Relevance of Information

Number of Cases	*Mean*	*Standard deviation*	*Standard error*	*t-*	*Significance of t*
Group 1(Expt.1) 54	14.1667	1.660	0.227	1.04	
Group 2(Control) 54	14.500	1.657	0.225		NS

Hypothesis 4.2

There is no significant difference between the post test mean scores of the achievement in methods of teaching physics of experimental group and the control group regarding the component of critical thinking skills namely determining the accuracy of a factual claim.

Table 4.23

Number of Cases, Standard Deviation, Standard Error, t-Value and a Significance of t of Post Test Mean Scores of the Experimental Group and Control Group Regarding the Control Group Regarding the Component of Critical Thinking Skills Namely Determining the Accuracy of a Factual Claim

Number of Cases	*Mean*	*Standard deviation*	*Standard error*	*t-*	*Significance of t*
Group1 (Expt.1) 54	14.1852	2.380	0.324	0.04	
Group2 (Control) 54	14.2037	1.956	0.266		NS

Since the computed value of 't' is less than the table value, the null hypothesis was accepted. This means that there is no significant difference between the post test mean scores of achievement in methods of teaching physics of the experimental group and the control group regarding the component of the critical thinking skills namely accuracy of a factual claim.

Hypothesis 4.3

There is no significant difference between the post test mean scores of the achievement in methods of teaching physics of experimental group and the control group regarding the component of critical thinking skills namely determining the credibility of a source.

TABLE 4.24

Number of Cases, Standard Deviation, Standard Error, t-Value and a Significance of t of Post Test Mean Scores of the Experimental Group and Control Group Regarding the Control Group Regarding the Component of Critical Thinking Skills Namely Determining the Credibility of a Source

Number of Cases	*Mean*	*Standard deviation*	*Standar d error d error*	*t-value*	*Significance e of t*
Group 1 (Expt.1) 54	14.8333	1.950	0.265	6.61	
Group 2 (Control) 54	14.9259	1.272	0.173		S**

Since the computed value of 't' is greater than the table value, the null hypothesis was rejected. This means that there is no significant difference between the post test mean scores of achievement in methods of teaching physics of the experimental group and the control group regarding the component of the critical thinking skills namely determining the credibility of a source.

Hypothesis 4.4

There is no significant difference between the post test mean scores of the achievement in methods of teaching physics of experimental group and the control group regarding the component of critical thinking skills namely identifying the unstated assumption.

Table 4.25

Number of Cases, Standard Deviation, Standard Error, t-Value and a Significance of t of Post Test Mean Ccores of the Experimental Group and Control Group Regarding the Control Group Regarding the Component of Critical Thinking Skills Namely Identifying the Unstated Assumption.

Number of Cases	*Mean*	*Standard deviation*	*Standard error d error*	*t-value*	*Significance e of t*
Group 1 (Expt.1) 54	7.1667	3.730	0.508	5.74	
Group 2 (Control) 54	10.7963	2.770	0.377		S**

Since the computed value of 't' is greater than the table value (at 0.01 level), the null hypothesis was rejected. This means that there is no significant difference between the post test mean scores of achievement in methods of teaching physics of the experimental group and the control group regarding the component of the critical thinking skills namely determining the credibility of a source.

Hypothesis 4.5

There is no significant difference between the post test mean scores of the achievement in methods of teaching physics of experimental group and the control group regarding the component of critical thinking skills namely determining the strength of an argument.

Since the computed value of 't' is greater than the table value (at 0.05 level), the null hypothesis was rejected. This means that there is no significant difference between the post test mean scores of achievement in methods of teaching physics of the experimental group and the control group regarding the component of the critical thinking skills namely determining the strength of an argument.

TABLE 4.26

Number of Cases, Standard Deviation, Standard Error, t-Value and a Significance of t of Post Test Mean Scores of the Experimental Froup and Control Group Regarding the Control Group Regarding the Component of Critical Thinking Skills Namely Determining the Strength of an Argument

Number of Cases	*Mean*	*Standard d deviation*	*Standar d error d error*	*t- value*	*Significance e of t*
Group 1 (Expt.1) 54	7.3889	4.109	0.559	2.33	
Group 2 (Control) 54	9.3519	4.634	0.631		S*

Hypothesis 4.6

There is no significant difference between the post test mean scores of the achievement in methods of teaching physics of experimental group and the control group regarding the component of critical thinking skills namely distinguishing statement of fact from value judgment.

TABLE 4.27

Number of Cases, Standard Deviation, Standard Error, t-Value and a Significance of t of Post-Test Mean Scores of the Experimental Group and Control Group Regarding the Control Group Regarding the Component of Critical Thinking Skills Namely Distinguishing Statement of Fact from Value Judgement

Number of Cases	*Mean*	*Standard deviation*	*Standar d error*	*t-*	*Significance e of t*
Group 1 (Expt.1) 54	17.6481	4.834	0.658	4.30	
Group 2 (Control) 54	21.2037	3.683	0.501		S**

Since the computed value of 't' is greater than the table value (at 0.01 level), the null hypothesis was rejected. This means that there is no significant difference between the post test mean scores of achievement in methods of teaching physics of the experimental group and the control group regarding the component of the critical thinking skills namely distinguishing the statement of fact from the value judgement.

Hypothesis 4.7

There is no significant difference between the post test mean scores of the achievement in methods of teaching physics of experimental group and the control group regarding all the components of critical thinking skills.

TABLE 4.28

Number of Cases, Standard Deviation, Standard Error, t-Value and a Significance of t of Post Test Mean Ccores of the Experimental Group and Control Group Regarding the Control Group Regarding All the Components of Critical Thinking Skills

Number of Cases	*Mean*	*Standard deviation*	*Standar d error*	*t-*	*Significance e of t*
Group 1 (Expt.1) 54	75.3704	10.555	1.436	6.06	
Group 2 (Control) 54	86.7963	0.989	1.223		S**

Since the computed value of 't' is greater than the table value (at 0.01 level), the null hypothesis was rejected. This means that there is no significant difference between the post test mean scores of achievement in methods of teaching physics of the experimental group and the control group regarding the component of all the critical thinking skills.

However the analysis indicates that, there is no significant difference between the post test mean scores of achievement in methods of teaching physics of the experimental group and the control group with respect to determining the relevance of information and determining the credibility of a source.

MAJOR HYPOTHESIS 5

There is no significant interaction between the nature of test, Sex, SES & intelligence regarding critical thinking skills based on an achievement in methods of teaching physics.

TABLE 4.29

Source of Variation, Sum of Squares, Degrees Freedom, Mean Square F value and Significance of F and Interaction Between the Nature of Test, Sex, SES and Intelligence Regarding the Component of C.itical Thinking Skills Namely Determining the Relevance of Information. (2 x 2 x 2 x 2 Factorial Design)

Source of variation	*Sum of squares*	*DF*	*Mean Square*	*F*	*Significance of F*
Main effects	16.759	4	4.190	1.510	NS
Test (pre-post) (A)	3.000	1	3.00	1.081	NS
Sex (B)	4.621	1	4.261	1.666	NS
SES (D)	1.894	1	1.894	0.683	NS
Intelligence (F)	9.276	1	9.276	3.344	S
2-way interactions	10.977	6	1.830	0.660	NS
Test Sex	2.352	1	2.352	0.840	NS
Test SES	1.298	1	1.298	0.468	NS
Test Intel.	0.190	1	0.190	0.068	NS
Sex SES	0.255	1	2.555	0.092	NS
Sex Intel.	0.008	1	0.008	0.003	NS
SES Intel.	6.004	1	6.004	2.164	NS
3-way Interactions	12.493	4	3.123	1.126	NS
A B D	0.001	1	0.01	0.00	NS
A B F	0.920	1	0.920	0.332	NS
A D F	0.077	1	0.077	0.028	NS
B D F	11.537	1	11.537	4.159	S*
4-way interactions					
A B D F	0.562	1		0.203	NS
Explained	40.791	15		0.980	NS
Residual	255.209	92			
Total	296.00	107			

Hypothesis 5.1

There is no significant interaction between the nature of

test, sex, SES & intelligence regarding the component of critical thinking skills namely determining the relevance of information.

From the above table it is evident that the obtained value of 'F' is less than the table value (0.05 level), hence the null hypothesis was accepted. However there is a significant interaction between sex, SES, and Intelligence regarding the component of critical thinking skills namely determining the relevance of information.

Hypothesis 5.2

There is no significant interaction between the nature of test, sex, SES & intelligence regarding the component of critical thinking skills namely determining the accuracy of factual claim.

TABLE 4.30

Source of Variation, Sum of Squares, Degrees Freedom, Mean Square F value and Significance of F and Interaction Between the Nature of Test, Sex, SES and Intelligence Regarding the Component of Critical Thinking Skills Namely Determining the Accuracy of Factual Claim

Source of variation		*Sum of squares*	*DF*	*Mean Square*	*F*	*Significance of F*
Main effects		20.806	4	7.201	1.606	NS
Test (pre-post) (A)		0.09	1	0.009	0.002	NS
Sex (B)		0.088	1	0.088	0.020	NS
SES (D)		16.715	1	6.715	1.497	NS
Intelligence (F)		23.355	1	23.355	5.207	S*
2-way interactions		28.247	6	4.708	1.050	NS
Test	Sex	7.271	1	7.271	1.621	NS
Test	SES	1.298	1	1.298	0.289	NS
Test	Intel.	0.616	1	0.616	0.137	NS

contd...

Source of variation	*Sum of squares*	*DF*	*Mean Square*	*F*	*Significance of F*
Sex SES	2.856	1	2.856	0.637	NS
Sex Intel.	3.988	1	3.988	0.809	NS
SES Intel.	9.762	1	9.962	2.221	NS
3-way Interactions	29.907	4	7.477	1.667	NS
A B D	13.068	1	13.068	2.914	NS
A B F	0.044	1	0.044	0.010	NS
A D F	2.974	1	2.974	0.663	NS
B D F	12.285	1	12.258	2.733	NS
4-way interactions					
A B D F	3.316	1	3.316	0739	NS
Explained	90.276	15	6.018	1.342	NS
Residual	502.917	92	4.485		
Total	296.00	107	4.700		

From the above table it is evident that the obtained value of 'F' is less than the table value (0.01 level), hence the null hypothesis was accepted. This means that there is no significant interaction between the nature of sex, SES, and intelligence regarding the component of critical thinking skills namely determining the accuracy of factual claim.

Hypothesis 5.3

There is no significant interaction between the nature of test, sex, SES & intelligence regarding the component of critical thinking skills namely determining the credibility of a source.

Since the computed value of 'F' is less than the table value (0.01 level), hence the null hypothesis was accepted. However, it is evident that there is no significant interaction between sex and intelligence regarding the component of critical thinking skills namely determining the credibility of a source.

TABLE 4.31

Source of Variation, Sum of Squares, Degrees Freedom, Mean Square F Value and Significance of F and Interaction Between the Nature of Test, Sex, SES and Intelligence Regarding the Component of Critical Thinking Skills Namely Determining the Credibility of a Source (2 x 2 x 2 x 2 Factorial Design)

Source of variation	*Sum of squares*	*DF*	*Mean Square*	*F*	*Significance of F*
Main effects	121.523	4	30.381	11.338	S**
Test (pre-post) (A)	118.231	1	118.231	44.123	S**
Sex (B)	0.044	1	0.044	0.016	NS
SES (D)	0.142	1	0.142	0.053	NS
Intelligence (F)	2.994	1	2.994	1.117	S*
2-way interactions	24.565	6	4.094	1.528	NS
Test Sex	0.828	1	0.828	0.309	NS
Test SES	4.013	1	4.013	1.497	NS
Test Intel.	0.186	1	0.186	0.069	NS
Sex SES	9.768	1	9.768	3.645	NS
Sex Intel.	4.180	1	4.180	1.560	NS
SES Intel.	10.859	1	10.859	4.053	NS
3-way Interactions	11.759	4	2.940	1.097	NS
A B D	13.068	1	1.456	0.543	NS
A B F	1.456	1	3.050	1.138	NS
A D F	1.72	1	5.304	1.979	NS
B D F		1	1.721	0.642	NS
4-way interactions					
A B D F	1.067	1	1.067	0.739	NS
Explained	158.914	15	10.594	1.342	S*
Residual	246.521	92	2.280		
Total	405.435	107	3.789		

Hypothesis 5.4

There is no significant interaction between the nature of

test, sex, SES & intelligence regarding the component of critical thinking skills namely identifying the unstated assumption.

TABLE 4.32

Source of Variation, Sum of Squares, Degrees Freedom, Mean Square F value and Significance of F and Interaction Between the Nature of Rest, Sex, SES and Intelligence Regarding the Component of Critical Thinking Skills Namely Identifying the Unstated Assumptions. (2 x 2 x 2 x 2 Factorial Sesign)

Source of variation	*Sum of squares*	*DF*	*Mean Square*	*F*	*Significance of F*
Main effects	434.258	4	108.564	10.140	S**
Test (pre-post) (A)	355.704	1	118.231	33.324	S**
Sex (B)	0.155	1	0.155	0.015	NS
SES (D)	73.831	1	73.831	6.896	S**
Intelligence (F)	0.059	1	0.059	0.006	NS
2-way interactions	69.818	6	11.636	1.087	NS
Test Sex	5.104	1	5.104	0.477	NS
Test SES	4.824	1	4.824	1.451	NS
Test Intel.	0.013	1	0.013	0.001	NS
Sex SES	52.588	1	52.588	4.912	S*
Sex Intel.	14.858	1	14.858	1.388	NS
SES Intel.	8.0203	1	8.0203	0.018	NS
3-way Interactions	5.787	4	1.447	0.135	NS
A B D	3.884	1	3.844	0.363	NS
A B F	0.091	1	0.091	0.009	NS
A D F	0.031	1	0.031	0.003	NS
B D F	1.510	1	1.518	0.142	NS
4-way interactions					
A B D F	5.120	1	5.120	0.478	NS
Explained	514.983	15	34.332	3.207	S*
Residual	984.980	92	10.706		
Total	1499.963	107	14.018		

Since the computed value of 'F' is greater than the table value (0.01 level), of the main effects, there is a significant difference among the main effects (nature of test), regarding the component of critical thinking skills namely identifying the unstated assumption).

From the above table it is also evident that the obtained value of 'F' is greater than the table value (0.01 level), hence the null hypothesis was rejected. Which means there is no significant interaction between sex and SES regarding the component of critical thinking skills namely identifying the unstated assumption.

Hypothesis 5.5

There is no significant interaction between the nature of test, sex, SES & intelligence regarding the component of critical thinking skills namely determining the strength of an argument.

TABLE 4.33

Source of Variation, Sum of Squares, Degrees Freedom, Mean Square F Value and Significance of F and Interaction Between the Nature of Test, Sex, SES and Intelligence Regarding the Component of Critical Thinking Skills Namely Determining the Strength of an Argument (2 x 2 x 2 x 2 Factorial Sesign)

Source of variation		*Sum of squares*	*DF*	*Mean Square*	*F*	*Significance of F*
Main effects		258.521	1	64.630	3.407	S*
Test (pre-post) (A)		104.037	1	104.037	5.484	S*
Sex (B)		6.201	1	6.201	0.327	NS
SES (D)		2.939	4	2.939	0.155	NS
Intelligence (F)		151.360	1	151.360	7.978	S**
2-way interactions		77.482	6	12.914	0.681	NS
Test	Sex	18.780	1	18.780	0.990	NS
Test	SES	21.446	1	21.446	1.130	NS
Test	Intel.	8.353	1	8.353	0.440	NS
Sex	SES	0.833	1	0.833	0.044	NS
Sex	Intel.	13.212	1	13.122	0.696	NS

contd...

Source of variation				*Sum of squares*	*DF*	*Mean Square*	*F*	*Significance of F*
SES		Intel.		19.911	1	13.212	1.050	NS
3-way Interactions				46.654	4	19.911	0.615	NS
A	B	D		0.110	1	11.663	0.006	NS
A	B	F		16.404	1	0.110	0.865	NS
A	D	F		8.476	1	16.404	0.447	NS
B	D	F		17.518	1	17.518	0.923	NS
4-way interactions								
A	B	D	F	9.127	1	9.127	0.481	NS
Explained				391.784	15	26.119	1.377	NS
Residual				1745.401	92	18.972		
Total				2137.185	107	19.974		

Since the computed value of 'F' is greater than the table value (0.01 level), of the main effects, there is a significant difference among the main effects with regard to the component of critical thinking skills namely determining the strength of an argument.

The computed value of 'F' is greater than the table value (0.05 level), for the pres test and post test scores. This means that there is a significant difference between pre test and post test scores with regard to the component of critical thinking skills namely determining the strengtht of a argument

From the above table it is also evident that the obtained value of 'F' is greater than the table value (for the interaction), the null hypothesis was accepted. This means there is no significant interaction between the nature of test, SES and intelligent regarding the component of critical thinking skills namely determining the strength of an argument.

Hypothesis 5.6

There is no significant interaction between the nature of test, sex, SES & intelligence regarding the component of critical thinking skills namely distinguishing statement of fact from value judgement.

TABLE 4.34

Source of Variation, Sum of Squares, Degrees Freedom, Mean Square F Value and Significance of F and Interaction Between the Nature of Test, Sex, SES and Intelligence Regarding the Component of Critical Thinking Skills Namely Distinguishing Statement of Fact from Value Judgement (2 x 2 x 2 x 2 Factorial Design)

Source of variation				*Sum of squares*	*DF*	*Mean Square*	*F*	*Significance e of F*
Main effects				258.521	1	64.630	3.407	S*
Main effects				395.333	1	98.839	5.148	S*
Test (pre-post) (A)				341.333	1	341.333	17.779	S**
Sex (B)				10.423	1	10.423	0.543	NS
SES (D)				0.661	4	0.661	0.034	NS
Intelligence (F)				40.246	1	40.246	2.096	NS
2-way interactions				97.815	6	16.302	0.849	NS
Test	Sex			0.085	1	0.085	0.004	NS
Test	SES			52.637	1	52.637	2.742	NS
Test	Intel.			0.328	1	0.328	0.017	NS
Sex	SES			4.618	1	4.618	0.241	NS
Sex	Intel.			4.655	1	4.6555	0.242	NS
SES	Intel.			31.968	1	31.968	1.665	NS
3-way Interactions				35.671	4	8.955	0.465	NS
A	B	D		1.9550	1	1.995	0.102	NS
A	B	F		5.066	1	5.066	0.264	NS
A	D	F		23.355	1	23.355	1.217	NS
B	D	F		5.494	1	5.494	0.286	NS
4-way interactions								
A	B	D	F	3.332	1	3.332	0.174	NS
Explained				532.175	15	35.478	1.848	NS
Residual				1766.232	92	19.198		NS
Total				2298.407	107	21.480		

Since the computed value of 'F' is greater than the table value (0.01 level), of the main effects, there is a significant difference among the main effects with respect to distinguishing statement of fact from value judgement.

The computed value of 'F' is greater than the table value (0.05 level), for the pres test and post test scores. This means that there is a significant difference among the main effects with respect to distinguishing statement of fact from value judgment.

Further it is evident from the table that the computed value (at 0.01 level), the null hypothesis was accepted. This means there is no significant interaction between the nature of test, SES and intelligent regarding the component of critical thinking skills namely distinguishing statement of fact from value judgment.

Hypothesis 5.7

There is no significant interaction between the nature of test, sex, SES & intelligence regarding all the components of critical thinking skills.

The computed value of 'F' is greater than the table value (0.01 level), for the pre test and post test scores. This means that there is a significant difference among the main effects with respect to all the components of critical thinking skills.

Further it is evident from the table that the computed value (at 0.01 level), the null hypothesis was accepted. This means there is no significant interaction between the nature of test, SES and intelligent regarding all the components of critical thinking skills.

From the above analysis it can be inferred that, there is a significant interaction bet sex, SES and intelligence the component namely determining the relevance of information. There is also significant interaction between SES and

TABLE 4.35

Source of Variation, Sum of Squares, Degrees Freedom, Mean Square F Value and Significance of F and Interaction Between the Nature of Test, Sex, SES and Intelligence Regarding all the Components of Critical Thinking Skills (2 x 2 x 2 x 2 Factorial Design)

Source of variation	*Sum of squares*	*DF*	*Mean Square*	*F*	*Significance of F*
Main effects	4469.919	1	1117.480	11.538	S**
Test (pre-post) (A)	3524.898	1	3524.898	36.395	S**
Sex (B)	0.112	1	0.112	0.001	NS
SES (D)	31.791	4	31.791	0.328	NS
Intelligence (F)	886.751	1	886.751	9.156	NS
2-way interactions	171.919	6	28.653	0.296	NS
Test Sex	22.960	1	22.960	0..237	NS
Test SES	0.124	1	0.124	0.001	NS
Test Intel.	37.351	1	37.351	0.386	NS
Sex SES	59.566	1	59.566	0.615	NS
Sex Intel.	49.674	1	49.674	0.513	NS
SES Intel.	24.484	1	24.484	0.253	NS
3-way Interactions	149.692	4	37.423	0.386	NS
A B D	6.326	1	6.326	0.065	NS
A B F	23.553	1	23.553	0.243	NS
A D F	11.887	1	11.887	0.123	NS
B D F	116.114	1	116.114	1.199	NS
4-way interactions					
A B D F	10.451	1	10.451	0.108	NS
Explained	4801.982	15	320.132	3.305	NS
Residual	8910.268	92	96.851		S*
Total	13712.250	107	128.152		

intelligence, sex and SES with respect to the components determining the credibility of a source of identifying the unstated assumption respectively. However there is no significant interaction between the nature of tests, sex, SES, and intelligence with respect to all components of critical thinking skills.

TABLE 4.36

Source of Variation, Sum of Squares, Segrees Freedom, Mean Square F Value and Significance of F Regarding the Achievement of Physics (2 x 2 x 2 x 2 Factorial Design)

Source of variation	*Sum of squares*	*DF*	*Mean Square*	*F*	*Significance of F*
Main effects	677.354	1	169.339	3.572	S
Sex (B)	29.104	1	29.104	0.614	NS
SES (D)	154.453	1	154.453	3.258	NS
Intelligence (F)	7.497	4	7.497	0.158	NS
CTS (N)	424.670	1	421.670	8.757	S
2-way interactions	201.821	6	33.637	0.709	NS
B D	44.562	1	44.562	0.709	NS
B F	61.016	1	61.016	0.940	NS
B N	5.063	1	5.063	0.107	NS
D F	64.855	1	64.855	1.368	NS
D N	5.063	1	3.053	0.064	NS
F N	64.855	1	0.264	0.006	NS
3-way Interactions	3.053	4	106.710	2.251	NS
B D F	0.264	1	2.509	0.053	NS
B D N	426.840	1	310.137	6.541	S
B F N	2.509	1	59.720	1.260	NS
D F N	310.137	1	10.672	0.225	NS
4-way interactions	10.672				
B F D N	165.785	1	165.785	3.497	NS
Explained	1471.800	15	98.120	2.069	NS
Residual	1801.700	92	47.413		NS
Total	3273.500	107	67.764		

MAJOR HYPOTHESIS 6

There is no significant interaction between sex, SES, & intelligence and critical thinking skills regarding the achievement in physics.

Since, the computed value of 'F' is greater than the table value (0.05 level), there is a significant difference between low critical thinking skills and high critical thinking skills with respect to achievement in physics.

It is also evident from that the computed value of F is less than the table (at 0.01 level), the null hypothesis was accepted. However, this means there is no significant interaction between sex, SES and thinking skills with respect to the achievement of physics.

Major Hypothesis 7

There is no significant difference between pre test and post test scores of the programme of critical thinking skills.

Hypothesis 7.1

There is no significant difference between pre test and post test scores of the programme of critical thinking skills regarding the component namely determining the relevance of information.

TABLE 4.37

Source of Variation, Sum of Squares, Degrees Freedom, Mean Square F Value and Significance of F Regarding the Critical Thinking Skills Namely Determining the Relevance of Information. (2 x 2 x 2 x 2 Factorial Design)

Source of variation	*Sum of squares*	*DF*	*Mean Square*	*F*	*Significance of F*
Explained	0.896	1	0.896	0.021	
Residual	2290.086	53	43.209		
Total	2290.982	54	42.429		NS

Since, the computed value of 'F' is less than the table value, the null Hypothesis is accepted. This means that, there is a significant difference between pre test and post test mean scores of the programme of critical thinking skills regarding the component namely determining the relevance of information.

It is also evident from that the computed value of F is less than the table (at 0.01 level), the null hypothesis was accepted. However, this means there is no significant interaction between sex, SES and critical thinking skills with respect to the achievement of physics.

Hypothesis 7.2

There is no significant difference between pre test and post test scores of the programme of critical thinking skills regarding the component namely determining accuracy the factual of claim.

Since, the computed value of 'F' is less than the table value, the null Hypothesis is accepted. This means that, there is a significant difference between pre test and post test mean scores of the programme of critical thinking skills regarding the component namely determining the accuracy of factual claim.

TABLE 4.38

Source of Variation, Sum of Squares, Degrees Freedom, Mean Square F Value and Significance of F Regarding the Critical Thinking Skills Namely Determining the Accuracy of Factual Claim

Source of variation	*Sum of squares*	*DF*	*Mean Square*	*F*	*Significance of F*
Explained	255.437	1	255.437	2.179	
Residual	6214.308	53	117.251		NS
Total	6469.745	54	119.810		

Hypothesis 7.3

There is no significant difference between pre test and post test scores of the programme of critical thinking skills regarding the component namely determining credibility of a source.

TABLE 4.39

Source of Variation, Sum of Squares, Degrees Freedom, Mean Square F Value and Significance of F Regarding the Critical Thinking Skills Namely Determining the Credibility of a Source

Source of variation	*Sum of squares*	*DF*	*Mean Square*	*F*	*Significance of F*
Explained	36.622	1	36.622	1.453	
Residual	1335.487	53	25.049		NS
Total	1372.109	54	25.490		

Since, the computed value of 'F' is less than the table value, the null hypothesis is accepted. This means that, there is a significant difference between pre test and post test mean scores of the programme of critical thinking skills regarding the component namely determining the credibility of a source.

Hypothesis 7.4

There is no significant difference between pre test and post test scores of the programme of critical thinking skills regarding the component namely identifying the unstated assumption.

Since, the computed value of 'F' is greater than the table value of F (at 0.05 level), the null hypothesis is rejected. This means that, there is a significant difference between pre test and post test mean scores of the programme of critical thinking skills regarding the component namely identifying the unstated assumption.

TABLE 4.40

Source of Variation, Sum of Squares, Degrees Freedom, Mean Square F Value and Significance of F Regarding the Critical Thinking Skills Namely Identifying the Unstated Assumption

Source of variation	*Sum of squares*	*DF*	*Mean Square*	*F*	*Significance e of F*
Explained	255.908	1	255.908	4.089	
Residual	3317.074	53	62.586		S**
Total	3572.982	54	66.166		

Hypothesis 7.5

There is no significant difference between pre test and post test scores of the programme of critical thinking skills regarding the component namely identifying the unstated assumption.

Since, the computed value of 'F' is greater than the table value of F (at 0.05 level), the null hypothesis is rejected. This means that, there is a significant difference between pre test and post test mean scores of the programme of critical thinking skills regarding the component namely identifying the unstated assumption.

TABLE 4.41

Source of Variation, Sum of Squares, Degrees Freedom, Mean Square F Value and Significance of F Regarding the Critical Thinking skills Namely Identifying the Unstated Assumption

Source of variation	*Sum of squares*	*DF*	*Mean Square*	*F*	*Significance e of F*
Explained	255.908	1	255.908	4.089	
Residual	3317.074	53	62.586		S**
Total	3572.982	54	66.166		

Hypothesis 7.6

There is no significant difference between pre test and post test scores of the programme of critical thinking skills with regard to the component distinguishing statement of fact from value judgment.

TABLE 4.42

Source of Variation, Sum of Squares, Degrees Freedom, Mean Square F Value and Significance of F Regarding the Programme of critical Thinking Skills with Regard to the Component Distinguishing Statement Cf fact from Value Judgement

Source of variation	*Sum of squares*	*DF*	*Mean Square*	*F*	*Significance of F*
Explained	1.626	1	1.626	0.093	
Residual	930.011	53	17.547		NS
Total	931.636	54	17.253		

Since, the computed value of 'F' is less than the table value of F, the null hypothesis is accepted. This means that, there is a significant difference between pre test and post test mean scores of the programme of critical thinking skills regarding the component with regard to the component distinguishing statement of fact from value judgment.

Hypothesis 7.7

There is no significant difference between pre test and post test scores of the programme of critical thinking skills with regard to all the components critical thinking skills.

Since, the computed value of 'F' is less than the table value of F (at 0.01 level), the null hypothesis is rejected. This means that, there is a significant difference between pre test and post test mean scores of the programme of critical thinking skills with regard to all the components critical thinking skills.

TABLE 4.43

Source of Variation, Sum of Squares, Degrees Freedom, Mean Square F Value and Significance of F Regarding the Programme of Critical Thinking Skills with Regard to all the Components Critical Thinking Skills

Source of variation	*Sum of squares*	*DF*	*Mean Square*	*F*	*Significance of F*
Explained	1.626	1	1.626	0.093	
Residual	930.011	53	17.547		NS
Total	931.636	54	17.253		

MAJOR HYPOTHESIS 8

There is no significant difference in the achievement in methods of teaching physics with respect to sex, SES, intelligence and critical thinking skills.

Hypothesis 8.1

There is no significant difference in the achievement in methods of teaching physics with of male and female teacher trainees.

TABLE 4.44

Number of Cases, Mean Scores, Standard Deviation, Standard Error, Value of t and Its Significance Regarding the Achievement in Physics of Male and Female Teacher Trainees

Number of cases		*Mean*	*Standard deviation*	*Standard error*	*t-value*	*Significance of t*
Group 1	16	56.3750	8.555	2.139	0.58	NS
Group 2	39	54.9487	7.623	1.221		

4(ii): Graph Indication the Mean Critical Thinking Scores Obtained by the Expereimental Group [Pre and Post Test Scores]

Since, the computed value of t is less than the table value of t, the null hypothesis is accepted. This means that, there is a significant difference between the achievement in methods of teaching physics of male and female teacher trainees.

Hypothesis 8.2

There is no significant difference in the achievement in methods of teaching physics of high and low SES teacher trainees.

TABLE 4.45

Number of Cases, Mean Scores, Standard Deviation, Standard Error, Value of t and Its Significance Regarding the Achievement in Physics of High and Low SES Teacher Trainees

Number of cases	*Mean*	*Standard deviation*	*Standard error*	*t-value*	*Signifi-cance of t*
Group 1 28	57.3214	7.508	1.419	1.80	
Group 2 27	55.5385	7.895	1.548		NS

Since, the computed value of t is less than the table value of t, the null hypothesis is accepted. This means that, there is a significant difference between the achievement in methods of teaching physics of high and low SES teacher trainees.

TABLE 4.46

Number of Cases, Mean Scores, Standard Deviation, Standard Error, Value of t and Its Significance Regarding the Achievement in Physics of High Low Intelligent Teacher Trainees

Number of cases	*Mean*	*Standard deviation*	*Standard error*	*t-value*	*Signifi-cance of t*
Group 1 36	55.7222	8.413	1.413	0.329	
Group 2 19	55.0566	6.655	1.569		

Hypothesis 8.3

There is no significant difference in the achievement in methods of teaching physics of high and low intelligent teacher trainees.

Since, the computed value of t is less than the table value of t, the null hypothesis is accepted. This means that, there is a significant difference between the achievement in methods of teaching physics of high and low intelligent teacher trainees.

Hypothesis 8.4

There is no significant difference in the achievement in methods of teaching physics of high and low critical thinking skills teacher trainees.

TABLE 4.47

Number of Cases, Mean Scores, Standard Deviation, Standard Error, Value of t and Its Significance Regarding the Achievement in Physics of High and Low Critical Thinking Skills of Teacher Trainees

Number of cases	*Mean*	*Standard deviation*	*Standard error*	*t-value*	*Significance of t*
Group 1 27	52.1481	5.895	1.134	3.25	
Group 2 28	58.4643	8.338	1.576		S**

Since, the computed value of t is greater than the table value of t, the null hypothesis is rejected. This means that, there is a significant difference between the achievement in methods of teaching physics of high and critical thinking skills teacher trainees.

MAJOR HYPOTHESIS 9

There is no significant difference between the total scores of critical thinking skills with respect to sex, SES, and intelligence.

Hypothesis 9.1

There is no significant difference between the male and female teacher trainees regarding their scores on critical thinking skills.

TABLE 4.48

Number of Cases, Mean, Standard Deviation, Standard Error, t Value and Its Significance of Male and Female Teacher Trainees Regarding their Scores on Critical Thinking Skills

Number of cases	*Mean*	*Standard deviation*	*Standard error*	*t-value*	*Significance of t*
Group 1 16	87.4375	8.366	2.092	0.38	
Group 2 39	86.4615	9.219	1.476		NS

Since, the computed value of t is less than the table value of t, the null hypothesis is accepted. This means that, there is a significant difference between the male and female teacher trainees regarding their scores on critical thinking skills.

Hypothesis 9.2

There is no significant difference between the high and low SES teacher trainees regarding their scores on critical thinking skills.

TABLE 4.49

Number of Cases, Mean, Standard Deviation, Standard Error, t Value and Its Significance of High and Low SES of Teacher Trainees Regarding their Scores on Critical Thinking Skills

Number of cases	*Mean*	*Standard deviation*	*Standard error*	*t-value*	*Significance of t*
Group 1 28	86..357	8.293	1.567	0.64	
Group 2 26	87.6154	9.782	1.918		NS

Since, the computed value of t is less than the table value of t, the null hypothesis is accepted. This means that, there is a significant difference between the high and low SES teacher trainees regarding their scores on critical thinking skills.

Hypothesis 9.3

There is no significant difference between the high and

low intelligent teacher trainees regarding their scores on critical thinking skills.

TABLE 4.50

Number of Cases, Mean, Standard Deviation, Standard Error, t Value and Its Significance of High and Low Intelligent Teacher Trainees Regarding their Scores on Critical Thinking Skills

Number of cases	*Mean*	*Standard deviation*	*Standard error*	*t-value*	*Significance of t*
Group 1 36	88.4167	9.643	1.607	2.17	
Group 2 18	83.5556	6.617	1.560		NS

Since, the computed value of t is less than the table value of t, the null hypothesis is accepted. This means that, there is a significant difference between the high and low intelligent teacher trainees regarding their scores on critical thinking skills.

QUALITATIVE ANALYSIS

Analysis based on the observation made by the researcher during the development of programme of critical thinking skills. The following details have been provided in the table no. 4.51.

Sub Programme 1: Meaning and Nature of Science

In this programme 90% of the trainees have scored 66.64% marks regarding all the questions, whereas the remaining 10% of the trainees scored more than this. This may be due to testing of the higher order mental processing. It was observed that in every group only two or three trainees dominated the discussion.

Sub Programme 2: Concepts and Principles

Under this programme, 90% of the trainees have scored 76.11% of marks by answering the questions regarding the

TABLE 4.51

Percentage of Scores Obtained Under Different Sub-Programme of C.T.S. Expressed in Terms of Different Percentile Points

P20	P30	P40	P50	P60	P70	P80	P90	P100	
8.33 0.50	16.66 1.00	24.99 1.50	33.32 2.00	41.65 2.50	49.80 3.00	58.31 3.50	66.64 4.00	74.97 4.5	P1
37.14 6.68	49.76 8.95	53.70 9.66	58.21 10.47	62.66 11.27	97.16 12.08	71.61 12.88	76.11 13.69	80.62 14.50	P2
36.60 4.76	41.98 5.46	47.37 6.16	52.75 6.86	58.29 7.58	63.51 8.26	68.90 8.96	80.12 10.42	93.81 12.20	P3
41.013. 18.90	45.57 21.00	49.36 22.75	53.16 24.50	65.83 30.34	69.35 31.96	72.86 33.58	78.12 36.00	85.71 39.5	P4
42.39 7.21	50.33 8.56	57.38 9.76	61.85 10.52	66.73 11.35	71.67 12.19	76.55 13.02	81.43 13.85	91.14 15.50	P5
30.34 5.16	34.33 5.84	38.39 6.53	40.74 6.93	46.45 7.9	50.50 8.59	54.50 9.27	67.62 11.50	85.26 12.01	P6
33.32 4.00	42.89 5.15	49.81 5.98	56.81 6.82	63.72 7.65	70.09 8.48	76.46 9.32	97.21 11.67	99.68 14.5	P7
17.6 4.80	23.32 5.83	27.4 6.85	31.56 7.89	35.56 8.89	40.72 10.16	51.88 12.97	54.00 13.50	78.00 19.5	P8
30.34 8.5	34.87 9.77	37.59 10.53	40.34 11.30	43.05 12.06	45.80 12.83	48.51 13.59	51.26 14.36	87.46 24.5	P9
19.31 5.41	22.02 6.17	24.77 6.94	27.48 7.70	30.23 8.47	32.95 9.23	38.30 10.73	45.05 12.62	51.76 14.5	P10
9.31 2.70	14.83 4.30	19.49 5.65	21.56 6.25	27.42 7.95	31.56 9.15	37.67 10.92	44.57 12.92	67.27 19.50	P11
37.98 5.70	43.02 6.47	48.15 7.23	52.74 7.92	58.40 8.77	63.93 9.60	77.78 11.68	91.70 13.77	96.27 14.50	P12
28.1 5.62	31.25 6.25	34.4 6.88	37.55 7.51	40.75 8.15	43.90 8.78	47.05 9.41	59.05 11.81	72.5 14.50	P13
21.90 5.69	26.02 6.76	31.99 8.31	37.22 9.67	44.27 11.50	51.32 13.33	60.09 15.61	71.87 18.67	94.32 24.50	P14
31.57 2.50	34.41 22.35	37.25 24.19	38.90 25.26	46.01 29.88	46.09 29.93	51.37 33.36	61.33 39.83	76.23 49.50	P15
	55.65. 56	61.4 6.41	67.2 2.72	73.1 7.31	78.90 7.89	84.70 8.47	90.50 19.05	95.00 9.5	P16

meaning of concept, principles and laws. Whereas 19.38% of the trainees could not attend the questions regarding identifying the concepts, facts, principles and laws in a given situation. Further they were not able to answer the questions regarding the application aspects of generalization and principles. This clearly indicates that most of the trainees have not been trained regarding the use of higher cognitive abilities. During the small group discussion, trainees have clarified their doubts which were not cleared at this stage were cleared later in the large group discussion. The involvement of trainees during the large group discussion was satisfactory.

Sub Programme 3: Scientific Method

In this programme, all the trainees have scored an average marks of 93.8%. Their performance regarding the classroom situation was good. Some of the questions regarding the appilcation of scientific method were not answered by the trainees (only 12% have answered). This may be due to lack of the opportunity for the trainees to solve the problems based on the scientific method. The trainees have participated actively both at the small group discussion and also at large group discussion.

Sub Programme 4: Scientific Attitude

Under this programme the performance of the trainees regarding teaching situations and questionnaire on scientific attitude was highly satisfactory (85.71%). Whereas the performance regarding the general situation was poor. However for all the questions related to the questionnaire and teaching situations, the trainees have discussed well. This may be because, as science students they have been trained regarding some of the components of scientific attitude through the curricular subjects. The participation of the trainees at the small group discussion level and large group discussion level was highly satisfactory. There was a gradual improvement in the participation of some of the trainees in the group.

Sub Programme 5: Inductive and Deductive Approaches

Under this programme questions which were asked to clarify the conceptualisation were answered properly. Whereas questions regarding comparing and identifying the ability of an approach in a given science situation were not answered by 8.86% of the trainees. This small and large group discussions helped the trainees to clarify their doubts.

Sub Programme 6: Inquiry Skills

In this programme, each member of the group was given a problem leading on the development of inquiry skills, 85.26% was the average score performed by the trainees. This indicates that 14.74% of marks were left out by the trainees. This is due to the difficulty level of questions like rearranging of the causes from most relevant to the least relevant and also to find the probable causes for the problem.

Sub Programme 7: Problem Solving

Under this program, each group was provided with a set of apparatus, using this the trainees have to solve a problem. After solving the problem questions were asked both at the lower level and at the higher level. The average scores obtained by the group was 99.68%. The smaller and larger group discussion helped them to do better in this programme. It has helped to increase the lower order and middle order cognitive process like identifying. 1. the alternatives, 2. related materials, 3. identifying the related rules, 4.suggestions to improve higher order mental processing including finding the solution to a problem.

Sub Programme 8: Models

In this programme all the trainees have answered about 75% of the questions testing lower order, middle order mental processing namely identifying the relevancy of the model no

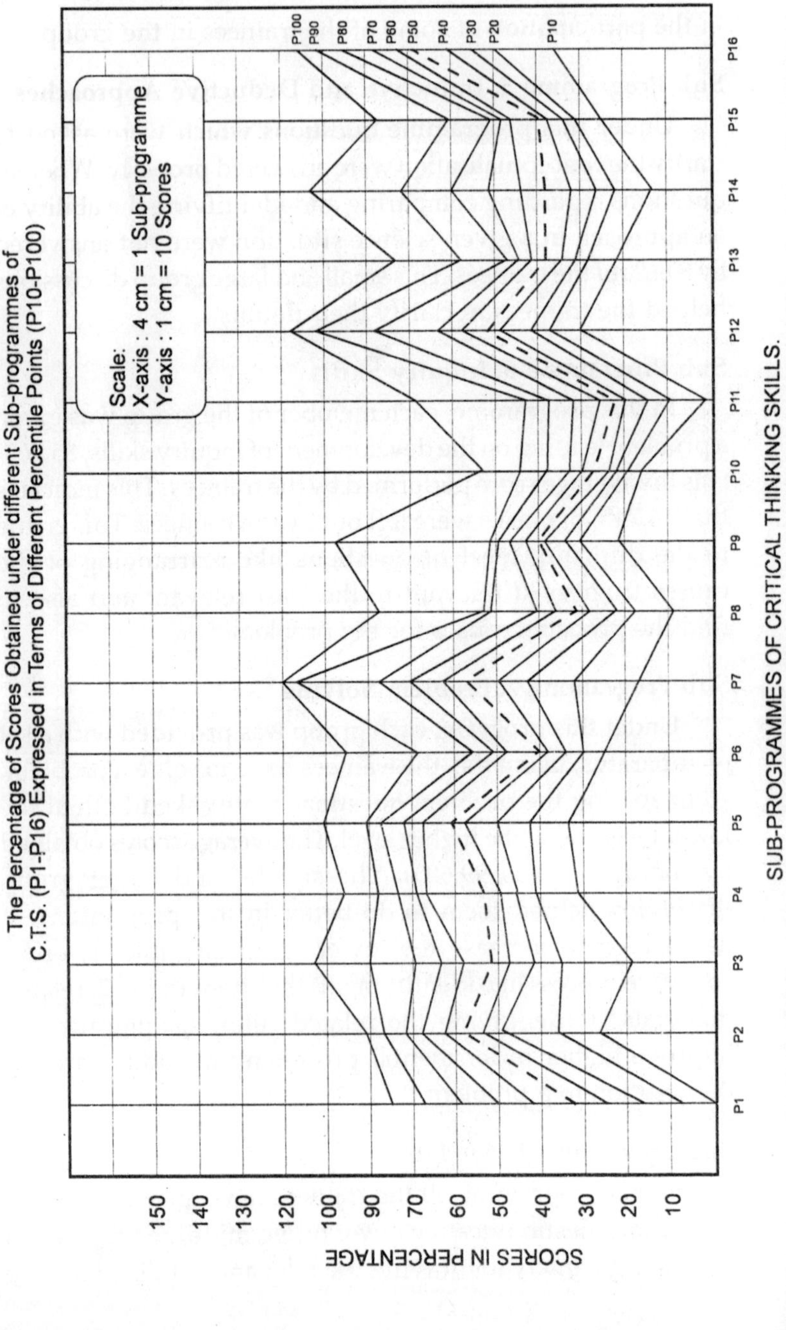
The Percentage of Scores Obtained under different Sub-programmes of
C.T.S. (P1-P16) Expressed in Terms of Different Percentile Points (P10-P100)
Scale:
X-axis : 4 cm = 1 Sub-programme
Y-axis : 1 cm = 10 Scores
P100
P90
P80
P70
P60
P50
P40
P30
P20
P10
P1
P2
P3
P4
P5
P6
P7
P8
P9
P10
P11
P12
P13
P14
P15
P16
SUB-PROGRAMMES OF CRITICAL THINKING SKILLS.
150
140
130
120
100
90
70
60
50
40
30
20
10
SCORES IN PERCENTAGE

factual accuracy, further around 12.01% of the trainees have not answered the questions. This may be due to the involvement of higher cognitive processing such as evaluation, suggestion to improve the existent models.

The discussion in the small group and also in the large group was found to be satisfactory.

Sub Programme 9: Resource Unit

In this programme, the average scores obtained by all the trainees has been found to be 87.46%. These are the scores obtained by the trainees by answering questions involving lower and middle order mental operations such as, 1. identifying the relevancy of the selected topic, 2. activity suggested were relevant are not.

About 12.54% of the trainees were not able to answer the questions involving the higher order mental abilities such as suggesions to improve the quality of the resource unit and evaluating its utilitarian values.

Overall the group discussion was satisfactory both at the small group and large group level.

Sub Program 10: Transparencies

Through this programme, the trainees were given set of transparencies to review. All the trainees have obtained around 51.76% only. This may be due to the difficulty level of the questions. All the trainees have found it difficult to identifing the suitability of the topic, the irrelevant of the diagram, the factual accuracy, coverage of essential point, suggesting different stages and modalities of using.

The smaller group discussion took more time when compared to larger group discussion to clarify the doubts regarding higher order questions.

Sub Programme 11: Science Club

During the programme all the trainees have scored 67.27% marks by attending to the questions which are testing lower and middle order mental abilities such as recognizing, relating and differentiating the objectives of the science club, where as regarding the identification of the relevance of evaluation and criteria for evaluation, most of the trainees (34.2%) have scored very low marks. This may be due to the lack of knowledge of the trainees regarding the criteria of evaluation.

Trainees have participated actively in the large group discussion when compared to the small group discussion.

Sub Programme 12: Field Trips

Under this programme, all the trainees have scored around 96.5%. This may be due to the reason that the knowledge and experience of answering the previous programme must have influenced this performance (similarity of the programme). However, some questions testing the higher order mental abilities like judging the sufficiency of objective and instruction before and during the programme were not answered by few trainees. There was not much scope for large group discussion.

Sub Programme 13: Science Magazine

In this programme, majority of the trainees (90%) have scored around 59.05% by answering the questions related to the lower and middle order mental abilities like identification of the relevant objectives and their sufficiency. Whereas questions testing the higher order mental ability were not answered by 40% of the trainees. This includes the judging the relevance of the title, authenticity of the people selected for evaluation etc.

Both smaller group discussion and larger group discussions were satisfactory.

Sub Programme 14: Evaluation

Under this programme, all the trainees have scored marks around 94.32%. Questions relating to lower and middle order questions like testing the ambiguity in questions, identifying the level of the objectives of the questions, identifying the relevance of alternatives etc. Only a small percentage of trainees did not answer the questions testing higher order cognitive processing such as determining the plausible items under alternatives based on reasoning. Group discussion were good.

Sub Programme 15: Reasoning Test

In this programme, all the trainees have scored marks around 76.23% by answering to questions based on observation and knowledge of the content. It was obvious that the scores obtained by them was due to the lower order mental ability. Questions testing the higher order cognitive ability were not answered by 35% of the students (including absurdity tests).

Both the small group and the large group discussions were focussed such as absurdity tests.

Sub Programme 16: Brain Storming

Under this programme, the researcher has noticed variations in the performance of students under different groups. Compared to the previous programmes all the trainees have taken part actively in the programme. Out of the two brain storming sections, performance of students in the second session was better when compared to the first. This may be due to the familiarity of the technique. All the trainees of different groups have scored around 95.5%.

The investigator also compared the scores of teacher trainees under different components of Critical Thinking Skills. It gives a clear idea that the scores at 50th percentile will be around 38.88% except for the compoent (Refer to graph no. 4.1).

Further, the different sub programmes of Critical Thinking Skills considered under five clusters shows that, clusters 1, 2, and 3 indicates the lower order mental operations, whereas clusters 4 and 5 indicates the involvement of higher mental operations. The scores obtained by the teacher trainees under different clusters also shows that they are consistent up to P50 in their marks under different clusters. (Refer to graph no. 4.5).

TABLE 4.52

Table Indicating the Inter Co-efficient of Correlation among the Six Components of Critical Thinking Skills

C1	C2	C3	C4	C5	C6	
C1	—	0.6612	0.6526	0.6226	0.6405	0.4479
C2	0.6612	—	0.5439	0.6103	0.7078	0.1905
C3	0.6526	0.5439	—	0.4784	0.7063	0.3836
C4	0.6226	0.6103	0.5484	—	0.6632	0.2896
C5	0.6405	0.7078	0.7063	0.6632	—	0.2287
C6	0.4479	0.1905	0.3837	0.2896	0.2287	—

GRAPH

From the above table it is evident that the co-efficient of correlation is high between the components C2, C5 and C3, C5. Whereas, the co-efficient of correlation is very low for the components C2, C6 and C5, C6. This clearly shows that the factual accuracy and the credibility of a source are mainly responsible in identifying the strength of an argument. Identifying the credibility of a source and strength of an argument involves higher mental processing.

The Scores of Five Trainees (Top)
under Different Components of C.T.S.

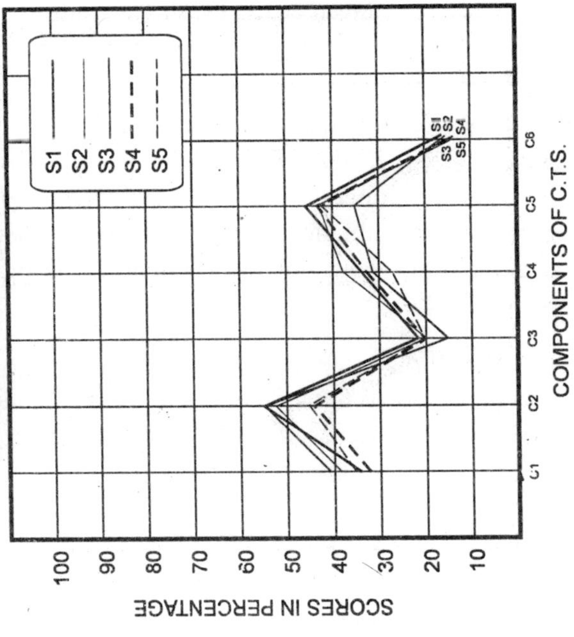

The Scores of Five Trainees (Low)
under Different Components of C.T.S.

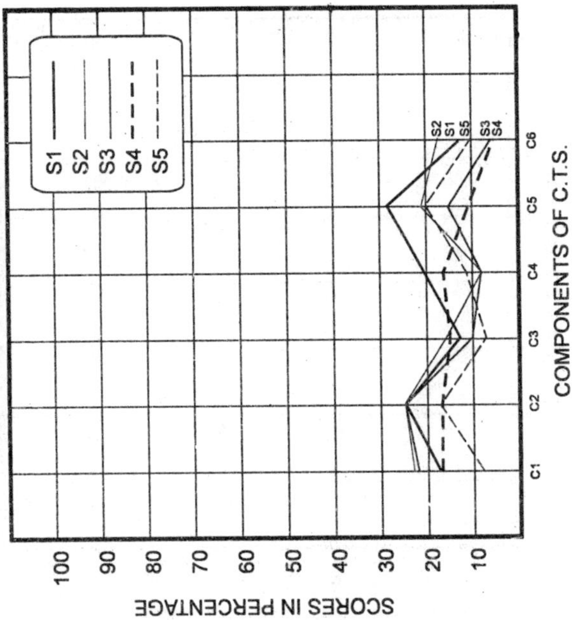

Student . No	C1	C2	C3	C4	C5	C6
Top Scorers						
1.	38	57	23	36	47	18
2.	39	54	22	39	43	17
3.	42	56	17	31	36	18
4.	34	47	21	34	43	14
5.	38	46	22	28	43	14
Low scorers						
1.	19	25	13	20	29	12
2.	22	25	17	09	21	15
3.	23	25	11	09	16	06
4.	18	18	15	16	11	06
5.	09	17	07	11	20	10
Mean Scores of All the Students						
	28.93	37.31	15.77	22.34	28.5	15.5

From the above table it is evident that the top five scores are consistent in their Critical Thinking Skills scores under different components. The poor performance of the low scores may be responsible for bringing down the Mean value of the various components of the Critical Thinking Skills. (Refer graph no. 4.6).

This the above chapter dealt with the analysis and interpretation of data. The summary and conclusion of the study will be discussed in the next chapter.

5

SUMMARY AND CONCLUSION

In the previous chapter analysis and interpretation of the data was discussed in detail. The present chapter contains summary and conclusion.

Introduction

The advancement of science and technology has brought many changes in all walks of life. The rapid expansion of knowledge, the innumerable number of gadgets are all the results of science. If science and technology is to be developed in the desirable direction, there is a need to focus on science education both at school and college level. This is essential because the quality of science education decides the quality of technological development. Therefore the responsibility of imparting quality science education depends mainly on science teachers.

The task of science teachers is not merely providing adequate knowledge and understanding about facts, principles and theories of science. In addition to this, their focus should be on developing scientific attitude and appreciation among the students.

In this direction the National Educational Policy – 1986(NEP), emphasizes more on developing the learner's abilities while teaching science. The policy highlights the quality of education in general and stresses more on quality improvement in science education.

Unless the spirit of inquiry, critical thinking ability, courage to question and aesthetic sensibility are developed among the students, the teaching of science becomes effective. Thus, the effective science teaching involves the information processing and development of cognitive abilities (as supported by Piaget, Kohleberg, Joyce and Weil etc.,)

In order to develop the various abilities and skills among the students, the science teacher should make sincere and consistent attempt in acquiring and developing these abilities in classrooms. Is it possible for a science teacher to develop these cognitive abilities among his students without he himself possessing them? As is the science teacher, so will be the science teaching and students learning.

Need for Study

The effective science teaching depends upon various factors such as teachers abilities and skills, teaching technique, prescribed content, nature of testing procedures, etc., Many studies are conducted in the area of finding the effectiveness of different methods of teaching such as Inductive – deductive approaches, Heuristic method, Problem Solving approaches etc. There are quite a number of studies dealing with the development of effective science curriculum at the secondary level (V.P Vardhini, M.J.Ravindranth, 1983, Malathi Seshadri, 1976).

Teaching of science at the secondary school level involves the teaching of concepts, scientific skills, phenomena theories and development of reasoning and psychomotor skills. In the process of teaching it is very essential to develop thinking and reasoning skills. According to Edward de Bono "thinking is a mental process it is a deliberate exploration of experiences for a purpose. The purpose may be understanding, decision

– making, planning, problem solving, judgement, action and so on..." Thinking is a skill which helps to perform any task efficiently in certain circumstances. Is thinking a skill that can be improved by practice and direct attention or is it an innate ability?. According to Ennis, Weddle and de Bono thinking is a learnable and also trainable ability.

Recently, much emphasis is given to the development of various cognitive skills such as analytical thinking, problem solving skills, creative thinking skills, critical thinking skills etc. There are many studies available where in they have given much importance for the development of creative thinking skills.

Like creative thinking, critical thinking is also very important in the teaching of SCIENCE. CRITICAL THINKING HELPS For BETTER information analysis, better evaluation which in turn may help the achievement of the students (Rosen 1986, Dorathy 1987, Edelman 1987). But regarding the area of critical thinking skills only a few studies are available related to science teaching at the secondary level. This may be due to the difficulty involved in pin-pointing the suitable situations in science and also the problem of quantifying the critical thinking skill.

If the science teacher really wants to modify the behaviour of his students and help them to develop scientific outlook, it is very necessary to process the critical thinking skills. This helps him to teach better which in turn helps the students to achieve better in their academic subject (Grief – 1961).

Teacher trainees have to do a lot of pedagogical tasks. In order to select and perform such tasks critical thinking is very essential. Further, it also helps them to organize their answers and to perform well in their academic subjects. If the prospective teachers possess this critical thinking skills, it may help them in turn to develop such skills among the students through their teaching. Since studies are not available in the area of science especially in physics at the training college level, the researcher has felt this as a need and hence the study.

Review of the Related Literature

The researcher has classified the reviewed related literature under two broader headings like the studies conducted in India and the studies conducted abroad. Regarding the studies conducted in India, the researcher has come across only a few studies related to the area of the present study namely critical thinking. However, there are quite a number of studies conducted in the area of cognitive abilities, cognitive processing, creative thinking, evaluation studies etc.,

Attempts are also have been made to test some of the cognitive abilities with respect to the studies conducted abroad, the researcher has come across quite a good number of studies. Among the studies reviewed, they have been classified under four different headings and namely:

(a) Studies related to conceptual clarity of critical thinking (Nancy 1990, Wright 1990, Snook)

(b) Critical thinking and related variables (Riesemmy 1991, Burt 1989, Batbs 1991...)

(c) Comparative and correlation studies on critical thinking (Banard 1979, Eckberg 1989, McGarrity 1990, Haboush 1989)

(d) Studies related to the development of critical thinking skills – implications of the above (Hudgins & Eddman 11986, Chemnalt 1989, Rile 1991, Fereell 1991..)

These studies helped the researcher to acquaint with the sampling technique, research design and also the rationale for selecting critical thinking skills as Independent variable

(Major variable, Elkino 1974, Kehler 1982, Rosn 1986, McGarriety 1990, Ryleigh 1991, Moreyra 1991).

Statement of the Problem"

"An impact of a programme of critical thinking skills on the achievement of Secondary school Teacher Trainees of Bangalore city."

Objectives of the Research

1. To develop a tool to measure critical thinking skills among the secondary school teacher trainees of Bangalore City.
2. To develop a programme of critical thinking skills based on methods of teaching Physics.
3. To study the impact of the programme of critical thinking skills on the achievement of Secondary School Teacher Trainees, in methods of teaching Physics.
4. To find out the interaction of Sex, Intelligence, S.E.S. and critical thinking skills on the achievement of Secondary School Teacher Trainees, in methods of teaching Physics.

Discussion of Variable

Based on the several studies conducted in the area of present research, the following are the variables selected.

(a) Critical thinking skills
(b) Sex
(c) Socio-economic status
(d) Intelligence
(e) Achievement.

Keeping the problem and the objectives of the study, the

above five variables were classified under Independent, dependent and Moderator variables.

Independent Variable:

Critical thinking skills.

Dependent Variable:

Achievement in methods of teaching Physics.

Moderator variable:

Sex, S.E.S and intelligence.

Operational Definitions

Programme

This means instructional programme based on the selected six components of critical thinking skills.

Critical thinking Skills

In this study critical thinking skills means the abilities to deal reasonably and reflectively with questions regarding clarification, inferring, investigation, making value judgment by establishing the relationship between previous experiences and the new situation.

The six components of the critical thinking skills that are suggested by Terry Applegate and Anitha Harnadek are considered. They are:

1. Distinguishing relevant from irrelevant information, claim or reasons.
2. Determining the factual accuracy of a statement
3. Determining the credibility of a source
4. Identifying unstated assumptions.
5. Determining the strength of an argument or claim

6. Distinguishing between verifiable facts and value claim.

Achievement

Achievement refers to performance of teacher trainees in the test of methods of teaching Physics.

Teacher Trainees

It refers to the students who are studying in different aided Colleges of Education come under Bangalore university offering B.Ed course (Bangalore city)

Sampling

In the present study the researcher was interested in finding the impact of critical thinking skills on the achievement of (methods of teaching physics) secondary school teacher trainees. Therefore, he has selected the colleges of education which are located in Bangalore City where the trainees who have taken methods of teaching physics were studying. Hence the present study involved purposive sampling technique. The size of the sample is 125, which included all the trainees who have taken methods of teaching physics as their methods.

Hypotheses

The following major and minor null hypotheses have been formulated keeping in mind the objectives and the variable under consideration.

Major Hypotheses

1. There is no significant difference between the pre test and post test mean scores of experimental and control group regarding critical thinking skills based on achievement in methods of teaching physics.
2. There is no significant difference between pre test and post test mean scores of the control group

regarding critical thinking skills based on achievement in methods of teaching physics.

3. There is no significant difference between pre test and post test mean scores of the experimental group and post test mean scores of the control group regarding critical thinking skills based on achievement in methods of teaching physics.
4. There is no significant difference between pre test and post test mean scores of the experimental group and the control group regarding critical thinking skills based on achievement in methods of teaching physics.
5. There is no significant interaction between the nature of test, sex, SES, and intelligence regarding critical thinking skills based on achievement in methods of teaching physics.
6. There is no significant interaction between sex. SES, intelligence and critical thinking skills based on the achievement in methods of teaching physics.]
7. There is no significant difference between pre test and post test scores of the programme of critical thinking skills based on the achievement in methods of teaching physics.
8. There is no significant difference in the achievement in methods of teaching physics with reference to sex, SES, intelligence and critical thinking skills.
9. There is no significant difference between the total scores of critical thinking skills with respect to sex, SES and intelligence.

Minor Hypotheses

Each of the first five major hypotheses was further analyzed into seven minor hypotheses keeping the different components of critical thinking skills (Chapter III) excepting sixth hypothesis which is on achievement in methods of teaching physics.

The seventh major hypotheses was further analyzed into seven minor hypothesis based on the different components of critical thinking skills.

The eighth major hypothesis was further analyzed into four minor hypothesis keeping the four variables such as sex, SES, intelligence and critical thinking skills.

Similarly the nineth major hypothesis was further analyzed into three more minor hypothesis keeping the variables sex, SES, and intelligence.

Tools Used for the Study

In the present study the investigator has selected Kuppuswamy's SES scale. This scale was modified suitably keeping the recent pay scales, later it was used to collect data regarding SES of teacher trainees.

To measure intelligence of the teacher trainees, the researcher has used Raven's Progresslive Matrices (RPM)

The investigator has prepared the achievement test based on physics content from B.Ed.syllabus following standardization procedure. This was used to collect data regarding the achievement in physics among teacher trainees.

Tools of Critical Thinking Skills (TOCTS)

The researcher has conducted a formal discussion meet with 30 experienced teachers to select the suitable components of critical thinking skills (using the 10 components given by Terry Applegate and Anitha Harnakek –1987). In addition to this, the researcher gave orientation to 30 B.Ed students regarding the different components of critical thinking skills. Later, they were given worksheets containing the sub units of the syllabus of methods of teaching physics. They were instructed to identify the components of critical thinking skills under each sub unit.

Based on the suggestions made by thinking experts, experienced teachers and B.Ed trainees the following six components of critical thinking skills were selected, namely:

1. Determining the relevance of information.
2. Determining the factual accuracy of a statement.
3. Determining the credibility of a source.
4. Identifying the unstated assumptions.
5. Determining the strength of an argument
6. Distinguishing between verifiable facts from value claims.

Under each of the above component, 15 items were constructed. Initially the critical thinking skills tool consisted of 90 items. These were given to five experts for validation (content and construct). Their suggestions were considered and the tool was further modified and refined.

Later the tool was tried out on a small group. Based on item validity, only 36 items were finally selected and the average time required to complete the tool was found to be 60 minutes. Tool was finalised based on the try out and item analysis. The reliability of the test has been found to be 0.83.

Developing the Programme of Critical Thinking Skills

The researcher has developed 16 sub-programmes related to the six components of the critical thinking skills. These sub programme were validated with the experts who are teaching the subject. As per their suggestions sub programmes were modified.

The sub programmes were prepared keeping the B.Ed

syllabus (methods of teaching physics). The programme developed by the researcher was give as treatment to the experimental group for a period of three months.(32 hours)

TABLE 5.1

Indicating the Details of the Programme of Critical Thinking Skills (POCTS)

Sl.No	*Programme*	*Media*
1.	Meaning of Science	Verbal
2.	Concepts and Principles	Verbal
3.	Scientific Method	Verbal
4.	Scientific Attitude	Verbal
5.	Inductive and Deductive Approach	Verbal
6.	Inquiry Skills	Verbal & Non-verbal
7.	Problem-Solving Approach	Verbal & Non-verbal
8.	Model	Verbal
9.	Resource Unit	Verbal
10.	Transparencies	Verbal
11.	Science Club Activities	Verbal
12.	Field Trips	Verbal
13.	Science Magazine	Verbal
14.	Unit Test	Verbal
15.	Reasoning Test	Verbal & Non-verbal
16.	Brain Storming	Verbal & Non-verbal

Research Design

The present study being partly developmental and partly experimental involving two types of design namely,

(a) Experimental and control group pre test and post test design

(b) Factorial design wherein each variable is varied at two levels to find out the interaction effect of these variable. Since the study involved four variables the design is 2x2x2x2 factorial design

Tools Used for Statistical Analysis

In the present study four ways analysis of variance, t – test and percentile ranks were used. In addition to this, correlation technique was also used to find out the inter-correlations among different components of critical thinking skills

Major Findings

1. There is a significant difference between the pre test and post test mean scores of experimental and control group regarding critical thinking skills based on achievement in methods of teaching physics.
2. There is no significant difference between pre test and post test mean scores of the control group regarding critical thinking skills based on achievement in methods of teaching physics.
3. There is a significant difference between the post test mean scores of achievement in methods of teaching physics of the experimental group and thinking controlled group regarding all the components of the critical thinking skills (Table 4.28).
4. There is no significant interaction between the nature of the test, sex, SES and intelliegence regarding all the components of critical thinking skills (Table 4.35).
5. There is a significant interaction between sex, SES and critical thinking skills with respect to achievement in methods of teaching physics (Table 4.36).
6. There is a significant difference between pre test

and post test scores of the programme of critical thinking skills regarding all the components of critical thinking skills (Table 4.43).

7. There is a significant difference in the achievement in methods of teaching physics of high and low critical thinking skills of teacher trainees (Table 4.47).
8. There is a significant difference between the achievement of high and low intelligent teacher trainees regarding their critical thinking skills (Table 4.50).
9. There is a significant difference between the pre test and post test mean scores of achievement in methods of teaching physics of experimental and control group regarding all the components of the critical thinking skills (with a special reference to the four components namely, determining the credibility of a source, identifying the unstated assumption, determining the strength of an argument and distinguishing statement of fact from value claim. (Tables 4.3, 4.4, 4.5 and 4.6.)
10. There is no significant difference between the pre test and post test mean scores of achievement of methods of teaching physics of control group regarding all the components of critical thinking skills. (Table 4.14), however, there is significant difference with respect to the two components namely, determining the credibility of a source and identifying the unstated assumption.(table 4.10 and 4.11 which may be attributed to either chance factor or the nature of teaching in the control group)
11. The scores obtained by the trainees in all the sixteen sub programmes were consistent. However, slight variation was due to the nature of the programme and the component of critical thinking skills.

12. The scores obtained by the trainees form p 10 to p 90 were consistent with respect to all the six components of critical thinking skills. however, it is comparatively loss for the two components namely determining the relevance of information and determining the factual accuracy of the statement.
13. The co-efficient of correlation is high between the component
    (a) Determining the factual accuracy of the statement and determining the strength of an argument (r =0.7078).
    (b) Determining the credibility of a source and determining the strength of an argument. (r =0.07063).

Major Conclusions

The study reveals that the programme of critical thinking skills (POCTS) has helped the teacher trainees improve their performance in critical thinking skills and achievement in methods of teaching physics as evident from post tests of (POCTS) as well as achievement test.

In other words, critical thinking skills has a significant impact on the achievement of teacher trainees in methods of teaching physics (Table 7.7. and 8.4).

Further, it was observed that intelligence was a significant factor in influencing the critical thinking skills of trainees. (Hypotheses 9.3). The socio-economic factor do not show any significant influence on the critical thinking skills.

The study also reveals that the Male and Female trainees do not differ in their critical thinking skills. This means, Sex has not influenced the critical thinking skills of teacher trainees. However, Sex, intelligence and SES have their significant interaction effect on critical thinking skills. Sex , SES and critical thinking skills also have their significant interaction effect on the achievement of teacher trainees in methods of teaching physics.

Among the six components selected, the following three components indicates more gain scores during treatment. They are:

C3 Determining credibility of a source.

C4 Identifying the unstated assumption.

C5 Determining the strength of an argument.

A glance at these components clearly indicates that they consitute higher cluster of cognitive abilities, which is very essential for a teacher of physics. It is interesting to note that the other three components of critical thinking skills namely:

C1 Determining the relevance of information.

C2 Determining the accuracy of a statement.

C6 Distinguishing between verifiable facts from value claim.

They do not show much significant impact on the achievement. This is perhaps, due to the fact that componentsC1, C2 C6 are prerequisites for the use fo components C3, C4 and C5 of the current methods of teaching physics syllabus has not lend itself for the emphasis of these components.

The different levels of group techniques adopted by the investigator helped in motivating the less expressive and inactive students to become more active and confident during discussion. Since critical thinking skills also helps in developing cognitive abilities and analytical ability, this in turn helps for broadening perspective and self improvement among the trainees.

Educational Implications

The study reveals that critical thinking skills being cognitive skills, are trainable. Therefore, there is a need to develop this skill. Curriculum experts should consider the different components of critical thinking while framing the curriculum. Even in the training programme structured group activities should be encouraged in the concerned subjects with reference to the different components of Critical Thinking Skills. Since Critical Thinking Skills will be having impact on the academic achievement of teacher trainees, at pre-service and inservice levels of education much emphasis should be given to the development of this skill. By developing improved programme for the teaching of thinking in general and critical thinking in particular, different models could be develop to suit the various levels of education. Critical Thinking Skills can be introduced while developing to suit the various levels of education. Critical Thinking Skills can be introduced while developing the curriculum. The educators can reduce the gap between what is known about thinking and how to teach it. This should be the effort of all teachers, teacher educators and educationists. The beneficiaries are not only the students but also the faculty as well as the society.

Limitations of the Study

1. The present study is restricted to the colleges of Education situated in Bangalore city only.
2. The study is limited to the trainees who have taken methods of teaching physics.
3. The programme of critical thinking skills involves more verbal tasks since it is content based.
4. Because of the nature of the course content, equal weightages for all the components of Critical Thinking Skills was not given while developing the programme.

Suggestion for Further Research

1. A comparative study could be undertaken involving urban and rural colleges of Education.
2. The present study can be extended involving the teacher trainees who have taken other branches of science of methods of teaching.
3. The study could be extending to the Secondary School level by including the other components of Critical Thinking Skills.
4. The study can be undertaken to identify some more components of Critical Thinking Skills.
5. A study can be undertaken for the construction and standardization of a general tool on Critical Thinking Skills.
6. There is a scope to develop a similar programme in vernacular.
7. The present study can be extended to find transfer of teaching by the teacher trainees in relation to critical thinking and achievement of students.

The structured programme of Critical Thinking Skills could be developed for inservice teachers teaching at school level.

BIBLIOGRAPHY

Beyer, Barry K., *Improving Thinking Skills—Defining the Problem,* phi-Delta Kappan, 1984, pp. 65-7.

Beyer, Barry K., *Developing a Thinking Skills Programme,* Allyn Bacon Inc., London, 1988.

Best, John, W., Kahn, James, V., *Research in Education,* Prentice-Hall of India Pvt. Ltd., New Delhi - 1, N 86, pp. 15-16, 217-219, 224-243, 265-267.

Bord, Walter B., *Educational Research: An Introduction,* David Moday, New York, 1967.

Bruner, S. Jerome, *The Process of Education,* Cambridge, Mass Harward University Press, 1963, Ch-I, p. 12.

Conway, Frade, *Sampling: An Introduction for Social Scientists,* George Allen & Unwin, London, 1967.

Burnett, R. Will, *Teaching Science in the Secondary School,* Holt, Rinehart and Winston, New York, 1960, pp. 218.

De Bono, Edward, *Teaching Thinking,* Penguin Books, New York, 1987.

Debono, Edward, *Lateral thinking: Creativity Step by Step.* Harper and Row, 1970, New York, pp. 15-28.

Dececco, John, P., Crawford, William, *The Psychology of learning and Instruction,* 2nd ed., Prentice-Hall Inc., New Delhi, N 88, pp. 39-40, 281-291, 303-311.

Dewey, John, *How We Think?,* D.C. Heath and Company, London, 1953.

Edwards, Allen *Techniques of Attitude Scale Construction,* Vakils, Faffer & Simpsons, Bombay, 1969.

Edwards, Allen, *Experimental design in psychological research,* Holt Rinchart and Winston, New York 1968,

Federer, T. Walter, *Experimental designs theory and application,* The MacMillan Company 1962.

Fox, David, J., *The Research Process in Education,* Holt- Rinehart & Winston, New York, 1963. Page 10-26.

Farmand, J. Galfo, *Interpreting educational research,* 3rd edn., W.M.C. Brown Company Publishers, USA. 1975, pp. 145-188.

Gayles, Richardson Anne, *Instructional planning in the secondary school,* David McKay Company Inc., New York 1973, pp. 9-120.

Gilbert, Sax, *Foundations of Educational Research,* Prentice Hall Inc., Englewood Cliffs, New Jersey, 1979. Karlinger, Fred N., Foundations of Behavioural Research - Educational and Psychological Inquiry, Halt-Riinenart & Winston, New York,

Goode, William, J. & Hatt Paul K., *Methods in social research,* McGraw Hill Kogakusha Ltd., New York, pp. 41-44, 132- 170.

Guilford, J.P., *Fundamental statistics in psychology and education,* McGraw Hill Book Company 1965.

Hitch Cock, David, *Critical Thinking - A Guide to Evaluating Information,* Methun publications, Canada, 1983.

Jepson, K.W., *Clear thinking* Longman Publication, 1962, pp. 3-5.

Joyce, Bruce, & Weil, Masha *Models of teaching,* Prentice- Hall of India Private Limited, New Delhi, 1985,

Kerlinger, Fred, M., *Foundations of behavioural research educational and psychological inquiry,* Halt Rinehart and Winston, New York, 1969, pp. 48-73.

Kurtz, Albert, & Mayo Samuel, T., *Statistical methods in education*

& psychology, Neroso Publishing House, New Delhi, 1980.

Linquist, E.F., *Statistical Analysis in Educational Research,* Oxford-IBM Publishing Co., New Delhi, 1970, pp. 48-72.

Marshall, Jon Clark, Hales, Loyde Wesley, *Classroom Test Construction,* Addisson-Wesley Publishing Co., Canada, 1971, pp. 173-233.

Nuffield Physics Questions, Nuffield foundation, Longmans / Penguin Books, Great Britain, 1967.

Popham, W. James, *Educational statistics* - use and interpretations, Harpa and Row Publisher, 1967.

Romiszowshi, A.J. (1984), *Producing instructional system,* Kogan page - London/Micholus Publishing, New York, Chapter 3-11.

Romiszoski, Alexander, J., *Producing Instructional Systems Lesson Plannings to Individualised and Group Learning Activities,* Kogan Page, London/Micholus Publishing, New York, 1984.

Rajeev, Garg, *World Famous Scientists,* Family Books Pvt. Ltd., New Delhi 1989.

Sucham, J.R. (1961), *Inquiry Training: Building Skills for Autonomous Discovery,* Merill-Palmer quarterly on behaviour development, vol. 7, pp. 147-169.

Travers, M.W. Robert (1969), *An Introduction to Educational Research,* third edition, Macmillan Publishing Company, Inc, London, pp. 299-316.

Ruckman, Wayne Bruce (1985). *Evaluating Instructional Programmes,* second edition, Allyn and Bacon Inc, London (985), pp. 171-198, 203-215.

Tuckman, Bruce N., *Conducting Educational Research,* Harcourt Brace, New York, 1972.

Tuckman Bruce, W., *Analysing and Designing Educational Research,* Harcourt Brace Jovanovich Inc., New York, 1979, pp. 15-33, 129- 149.

Vaidya, Narendera, *The Growth of Logical Thinking in Science during Adolescence,* Oxford-IBM Publishing Co., New Delhi, 1972.

Nathan, S. Washton, *Teaching Science Creatively,* Saunders science teaching series, W.B. Saunders Company, London, 1967, pp. 33-42, 217-248.

Wiersma, William, *Research methods in education: an introduction* -fourth edition, Allyn and Bacon Inc, London, 1986, p. 23, 43, 101-279.

Yadva, M.S. and Shiv K. Mitra (1989), *Educational Research - Methological Centre for Advanced Study in Education Perspectives,* The M.S. University of Baroda, Baroda, pp. 256- 260.

Torrence, E. Paul, *Guiding creative talent.* Prentice Hall International Inc., p. 5-20.

JOURNALS & ENCYCLOPEDIA

Baldwin, Dorathi, "The effects of two instruction methods on critical thinking". *Dissertation Abstract International,* Vol. 48, September 1987, Page No. 2142.

Bates, Dorothy Schwleckardt, "Effect of a systematic inquiry intervention on the critical thinking skills of a sample of master's degree students". *Dissertation Abstracts International.* Vol. 52 No. 9, March 1992.

Bryce, B. Hudgins Sybil Edelman; "Teaching critical skills to fourth and fifth graders through Teach-led-small-group discussions". *The Journal of Educational Research.* Vol. 79, July/August, 1986, No. 6.

Bryce B. Hudgins Sybil Edelman (1988). *"Children's self-directed critical thinking". The Journal of Educational Research,* Vol. 81, May/June, No. 5.

Burt, Charles Wesley, "Identification of critical variables in developmental testing and an experimental examination of the number and roles of participants in testing sessions". *Dissertation Abstracts International,* Vol. 50, No. 4, October 1989.

Candac, Elaine, "The effects of literary discussion groups on students critical thinking ability and attitude towards reading", *Dissertation Abstracts International,* Vol. 52, No. 5, November 1990.

Chennault, Anita (1989). *"Enhancing critical thinking skills in gifted elementary school students". Dissertation Abstracts International.* Vol. 50, No. 4, October 1989,

Das, P., *"Structure of cognitive abilities among normal and tribal children as a function of developmental leve". Fourth Survey of Educational Research,* (Ed: Buch, M.B.) NCERT, New Delhi, N85, pp. 358-359.

De, B., "Cognitive style ability of tribal and non-tribal school pupils", *Fourth Survey of Educational Research* (Ed: Buch, M.B.), NCERT, New Delhi, N85, pp. 359-360.

Deshpande, M.B., *"An analytical study of cognitive-affective development and scholastic achievement of tribal secondary school students", Fourth Survey of Educational Research,* (Ed: Buch, M.B.), NCERT, New Delhi, N84, pp. 360.

Eckberg, Ernest Daniel, "Perception of control of environment and its relation to the acquisition of critical thinking and conflict resolution skills", Dissertation Abstracts International, Vol. 50, No. 12, June 1990.

Edward W, Smith et. al., *"The educators encyclopedia"*, Prailice Hall Inc., Englewood chief, N.J., pp. 612-618.

Ennis, Robert, *"A conceptof critical thinking"*, Harward Educational Review, Vol. 32, l,Winter 1962, pp. .81.

Farrell, Susan Daughtry. *"Critical thinking as a function of teacher" questions. Dissertation Abstracts International.* Vol. 52, No. 9, March 1992.

Gage, M.L. *Handbook of Research on teaching, American Educational Research Association,* Rand Mc Malley and Co., Chicago, 1963.

Hahough, Karen Lynn., *"An evaluation of student learning outcomes under a critical thinking-social studies program". Dissertation Abstracts* International, Vol. 50, No. 10, April 1990.

Harris W. Chester and Liba R. Marie (Ed), *"Encyclopedia of educational research-third edition",* The Mac Millan Company, New York, 1960, P408, 645.

Huesken, Gerald George. *"The relationship between principals self-perceived leadership in the teaching of critical thinking skill and students"* Dissertation Abstracts International. Vol. 50, No. 6 Jan 1991.

Ircink Waite, Ruth Margueria, *"A measurement of critical thinking in senior baccalaureate nursing students", Dissertation Abstracts International,* Vol. 50, No. 11, May 1990.

John Follman, *"Representative critical thinking correlations" : Reprised journal of educational research and extension,* Vol. 29, No. 2, October 1992.

Johnson, Lynn Nations, *"Learning to be a responsive teacher : Assisting student performance during class discussion to enhance critical thinking", Dissertation Abstracts International,* Vol. 50, No. 8, February 1990.

Jordon, Cynthia, *"The relationship among reading comprehension, critical thinking, and me - comprehension and the effects of?netacomprehensive strategic training". Dissertation Abstracts International.* Vol. 51, No. 7, January 1991.

Kezar, Lois Paulson *"Effects of computer technology and traditional methods of instruction upon the critical thinking skills of teachers and students". Dissertation Abstracts International.* Vol. 52, No. 8, February 1992.

Lipman, Mathew, *"Critical thinking "What it aims", Educational leadership.* May 1985.

Mc Gurrity, Linda Jenn, *"A study of the relationship of academic acheivement, program preparation, critical thinking ability, and classroom performance of pre-service teachers in two selected Universities in Georgia", Dissertation Abstracts International,* Vol. 51, No. 5, November 1990.

Michael Eravt (Editor), *"The international encyclopedia of educational technology"*, pergamon press, Oxford, 1989, pp. 27-29.

Michael J. Dunkin (Editor). *"The international encyclopedia of teaching and teacher education"*, Pergamon Press, New York, pp. 380- 89 1987.

Mitzel E. Harold (Editor in chief), *"Encyclopedia of educational research"* fifth edition, Vol. 4, Sponsored by the American Educational Research Association,

Moreyra, Alicia Amalia, *The role of thinking frames in developing teachers' critical thinking skills and dispositions. Dissertation Abstracts International.* Vol. 52, No. 7, January 1992.

Pandey, Ashok Kumar. *Divergent thinking in relation scholastic acheivement, cognitive style, self-concept and interest pattern, Indian Educational Review,* Vol. 27, No. 1, January N92, NCERT, New Delhi, pp. 560-60.

Provaznik Ebel, Debra, *"Analysis of teachers' and children's verbal behaviour, self-directed critical thinking small-group discussion", Dissertation Abstracts International.* Vol. 52, No. 6, December 1991.

Ray, P, "Effects of Attribution Training on the Development of Intellectual Acheivement, Responsibility and Cognitive performance among lower class children",

Fourth Survey of Educational Research, (Ed: Buch, M.B.) NCERT, New Delhi, N82, pp. 423.

Riley, Vera Maxine, "Teachers' questioning for improvement of critical thinking skills", *Dissertation Abstracts International,* Vol. 53, No.3, September 1992.

Risenmy, Dadonna Rose, "Retention and transfer of children's self-directed critical thinking". *Dissertation Abstracts International,* Vol. 52, No. 6, December 1991.

Rogers, Gloria, Martin *"Critical thinking and Intellectual development: A study of the effects of an integrated first year curriculum in science, engineering and mathematics". Dissertation Abstracts International,* Vol.52, No. 9, March.

Sundep. P., "Classroom interaction and cognitive development in primary school children", Third Survey of Educational Research, (Ed: Buch, M.B) NCERT, New Delhi, N79, pp. 405-406.

Silverstein Jan. E., "Classroom interactions and critical thinking ideals, self perceptions and actions". *Dissertation Abstracts International,* Vol. 50, No. 12, June 1990.

Song, Yong. "The relationship between elementary school teachers and students cognitive questioning preferences and students achievement", *Dissertation Abstracts International,* Vol.43, No. 3, 1982, P. 656.

Stahl, Nancy Nance, Developing criteria for a critical thinking program using the Delphi technique. *Dissertation Abstracts International,* Vol. 51, NO.7, January 1991.

Husen Torsten and Portlethwaite T. Nevile , *The International Encyclopedia of Education,* Vol. 8, Oxford/New York 1985, pp. 4461-4464, 1985.

Traverse, Robert M.W. *(Ed.), Second Hand Book of Research on Teaching": A project of the American Reserach Association,* Rand-McNelly College Publishing Co., Chicago, 1973, pp. 21-51.

Treece, Suzanne S., "An Experimental Study of the Effects if Hannel's Cognitive Educational Program for primary school children with measurement of achievement and cognitive skills", *Dissertation Abstracts International,* Vol. 50, No. 12, June 1990, pp. 384A.

INDEX

❑❑❑